CRESTLINE

C H R O N I C L E S

CRESTLINE
C H R O N I C L E S

Rhea-Frances Tetley

Charleston London

THE
History
PRESS

Published by The History Press
Charleston, SC 29403
www.historypress.net

Front cover, top: Toboggans were not only used for recreation but were also a popular mode of transportation in Crestline's early years. *Bottom*: The creation of Lake Gregory in the 1930s has transformed Crestline into a year-round tourist destination.

Back cover, top: The beautiful Club San Moritz Lodge in the 1960s. *Bottom*: Archery was a popular activity at the Arrowhead Valley Club in the 1920s.

First published 2012

Manufactured in the United States

ISBN 978.1.60949.584.8

Library of Congress CIP data applied for.

CONTENTS

CONTENTS

FOREWORD

F ew persons are intimately acquainted with and connected to Crestline's past more than Rhea-Frances Tetley, granddaughter and great-granddaughter of Valley of Enchantment subdividers and developers Frank A. Tetley Sr. and Frank A. Tetley Jr. (Tetley & Son). While Charles S. Mann and Arthur Gregory were carving out the subdevelopments that would become Crestline proper, Tetley & Son was engaged in developing Rim of the World Park, which would later become known as Valley of Enchantment.

Though born and raised in Whittier, California, Rhea-Frances spent many weekends and summers visiting her family's log cabin vacation home on Tetley Lane (a former sales office for the Valley of Enchantment subdivision) in Crestline. It was during these childhood visits that she explored the surrounding forest, lakes and streams, fell in love with the mountain area and vowed to someday reside there.

Rhea-Frances's childhood dream came true in July 1976, when she and I, upon our return from a six-month-long bicentennial tour of the United States, during which we lived out of our Volkswagen minibus, decided to settle down in the family cabin and raise a family of our own. We had been college sweethearts (it was love at first sight...and still is) who had met at Chapman College (now Chapman University) in Orange, became engaged after graduation and were married in 1973.

It was during early childhood family gatherings that Rhea-Frances learned, firsthand, from her father, grandfather and great-aunt about the various stages of the development of Valley of Enchantment and its mutual water company. This only whetted her appetite for learning more about history and led her to acquire a BA in history and a subsequent MA in education so she could disseminate what she had learned. Ever inquisitive, it wasn't long after we settled here in 1976 that she continued her quest for history by striking up friendships with some of Crestline's still-living pioneers and compiling their recollections into a series of historical articles in several local publications.

Rhea-Frances's thirst for historical facts led to her co-founding of the Crest Forest Historical Society in 1986 and the creation of an oral history project, in which a series of in-depth interviews with still-living area pioneers was tape-recorded and preserved for the benefit of future generations. In 1997, the Crest Forest Historical Society expanded its area of historical interest and became the Rim of the World Historical Society.

In addition to writing historical and general news articles for the *Crestline Chronicle* and *The Alpenhorn News* since 2001, as well as authoring two books on local history, over the years, Rhea-Frances Tetley has served as president and board member for both the Crest Forest and Rim of the World historical societies, as a founder and president of Soroptimists International of Crestline and as presiding officer of several Masonic organizations. Oh, and in her spare time, she also teaches learning-handicapped sixth, seventh and eighth graders in Redlands. And the rest is, as they say, history.

Douglas W. Motley
Senior Writer for *The Alpenhorn News*

Acknowledgements

There are several people who are directly responsible for the development of this book. Most important would be my family, who freely shared their stories of the mountains and its development with me during family visits to both the mountains and the Tetley family homes in Riverside, California, including my aunt Frances Tetley Harthan and grandfather Frank Tetley Jr. Both of my parents, Richard and Ruth (Harper) Tetley, vacationed in the Crestline area as children and have often shared their childhood experiences with me, even when I was a child and didn't yet care.

My thanks go to Crestline's former honorary mayor, Tom Powell Jr., who involved me in the formation of the Crest Forest Historical Society because it tapped into my knowledge and interest in local history, which was stimulated by Chapman College professor Dr. James Utter.

The many members of the Crest Forest and Rim of the World Historical Societies who have encouraged my newspaper history writings over the past twenty-five years and who have shared their research and knowledge are an integral part of this book. Their collections and writings, and our work together in building the various Mountain History Museums, have added greatly to my body of knowledge. I want to thank all the past presidents and longtime members for their support. Most of all, to my personal friend Pauliena LaFuze, who did all the detailed and documented research into the early history of the mountains, personally encouraged me to write about Crestline and corrected my facts when needed (but always in the most polite way ever), I owe a great debt.

Dennis Labadie, the owner and publisher of the *Crestline Chronicle* and *The Alpenhorn News*, saw the value of publishing a history article on the mountain communities from the first issue of his newspaper and has encouraged me to document the people, events and locations of local history. Without him, none of these articles would have ever been written. I thank him for allowing me to write so many hundreds of thousands of words for his newspapers over the past eleven years. It has been a wonderful experience.

Lastly, my family, sons David and Sean Motley, who have listened to me spout endless historical factoids until their eyes glazed over, I thank you for your support, tolerance and computer knowledge. To my husband of almost forty years, Douglas Motley, who has edited my newspaper columns, supported my historical vision and much more over the years, I greatly appreciate your love, support and devotion, especially when my tenses don't match.

INTRODUCTION

Crestline is the first town at the crest of the San Bernardino Mountains in Southern California. These mountains separate the coastal plain from the deserts, stopping much of the coastal moisture from reaching the deserts beyond and creating the tall cedar pine and oak forest that grew on the summit.

Indians used these mountains for hundreds of years during the summer as a retreat from the hot desert sun (where the Mojaves spent their winters). The mountains' 4,300- to 11,000-foot elevations had cool breezes through the pines and a plentiful food supply of nuts, acorns, berries and wild game. The meadows and streams of Valley of Enchantment, Arrowhead Highlands, Dart Canyon and many other locations have evidence of many generations of Indian encampments.

The Mormon loggers in the 1850s were the first white men to enter the pristine forests, other than crossing over the mountains like mountain man Jedediah Smith in 1826, chasing renegade Indians like Benito Wilson when he discovered the Big Bear area in 1845 or taking a short trip into the lower elevations to cut firewood like Juan Bandini during the Spanish era. The Mormons cut the trees for lumber to sell in the growing community of Los Angeles to pay off the mortgage on the land, which they had purchased from the Lugo family. That settlement became the town of San Bernardino. West Twin Creek (later Waterman) Canyon was the most direct route to the crest, and that crest/top area eventually became the community of Crestline.

There are many strong personalities who shaped the community just by living or working there, such as David Seely, Arthur Gregory, Samuel Dillin,

INTRODUCTION

John Adams, Charles Mann and Rose Allen. Each has a story explaining his or her part in changing the landscape and growing the community. The establishment of the San Bernardino National Forest in the 1890s changed the emphasis from lumbering to recreational use of the land, and the continued private ownership of land within the forest boundaries has made it the most densely populated forest west of the Mississippi River and with the most visitors. This unique area has seen many changes over the years.

This book includes some of the stories of those early years, as published by newspaper owner/publisher Dennis Labadie from 2001 through 2011, initially in the *Crestline Chronicle* and then in *The Alpenhorn News*, both San Bernardino Mountain newspapers. Several important stories are recounted from a couple different perspectives as those events affected several different aspects of the community at the time, including the 1911 fire, the roads and Paradise Gulch.

I
COMING TO THE
MOUNTAINS

WATERMAN CANYON

Crestline is at the northern upper end of Waterman Canyon in the San Bernardino Mountains of Southern California. Waterman Canyon has been an entrance to the San Bernardino Mountains from the valley floor since the days when the Spanish knew the mountains as the "Sierra Nevadas" or "Sierra Madre."

In centuries prior, the Indians had discovered the now-named Arrowhead Hot Springs in the foothills above the valley and used the water's curative powers for hundreds of years. Church records document that Father Joaquin Nunez frequented the "Agua Caliente," the Spanish name for those hot springs, in 1820.

Initially called Twin Creek Canyon by the Mormons, it was the route used to construct their road up to the trees they could see on the mountaintop. The whole Mormon colony worked together in a community project to build a narrow dirt road up the canyon in 1853. The men and women of the colony spent ten days and one thousand man-hours building the Mormon Lumber Road to the crest. At some stretches of the road near the summit, it had a 49 percent grade. The trees were harvested and milled into lumber and transported down the mountain, where they were sold to pay for the purchase of the land for the colony in San Bernardino.

The road was washed out during the 1862 Noachian Flood because an approximately one-mile-wide segment of the crest drains into the single creek in the narrow canyon. The logging road was repaired for the loggers to

A steaming hot spring is a natural feature in Waterman Canyon.

use, but it remained a steep and dangerous roadway. After the second flood in 1867 ruined the road completely, it was not rebuilt, and routes through other canyons, such as Daley Canyon and Devil's Canyon, were constructed.

Waterman Canyon is named for Robert Whitney Waterman, who had a home and ranch at the mouth of the canyon for several decades of the late 1800s. Waterman became California's governor while living there. He came to California twice from Illinois, first to Northern California during the California gold rush and later with his family to live in San Bernardino. He and a partner discovered silver and started the silver rush near Calico with his Waterman Silver Mine. He was elected California's lieutenant governor in 1886 and became governor in 1887, when Governor Washington Bartlett died. Due to poor health, Waterman did not run for reelection. He returned to San Bernardino and died in San Diego in 1891.

Because Waterman recognized the purity and uniqueness of the water on his property, he refused to allow anyone to use the washed-out Mormon

Coming to the Mountains

Logging Road, which traversed his property to access the mountaintop. After his death, the Arrowhead Reservoir Company was able to get a contract to build its Arrowhead Reservoir Toll Road to transport construction equipment and bags of cement up to the summit for the massive seven-lake irrigation project it was building in the San Bernardino Mountains. Waterman had been a great proponent of water projects during his term as governor, so the family allowed the road to be constructed after his death.

The San Andreas Fault, located at the base of the mountains, creates the hot springs. The constant movement of the fault creates the heat of the springs. According to a pamphlet published just after the third Arrowhead Hot Springs Hotel was constructed, the springs "escape from enormous depths, beyond possibility of contamination, where either active volcanic changes are taking place or the layers of the earth's crust are crushing and grinding against each other at enormous pressures with production of heat."

The area received the name Arrowhead from the unique scar on the mountain face, seven and a half acres in size. Over the years, it had many nicknames, including the "Ace of Spades," but Indian legends and the romance of the discovery of the hot springs and steam caves used by both the Indians and David Noble Smith made it seem like the scar was pointing to the hot springs at its base. Four hotels have been built at the hot springs site over the years.

The entrance to Waterman Canyon is seen, looking north, past the Arrowhead Spring Hotel and Arrowhead landmark.

There are three distinct hot springs in the canyon that were developed for the Arrowhead Springs Hotel. The Penyugal Spring was claimed to be the hottest developed curative hot spring in the world at 196 degrees Fahrenheit. Penyugal Springs had sixty-seven grains per gallon of natural salts in the water, including sodium sulfate, sodium chloride, silica, potassium sulfate and calcium carbonate, with smaller amounts of magnesium, sodium and hydrogen sulfide gas.

Granite Spring had a temperature of 152.6 degrees with fifty-seven grains of salts per gallon. The Palm Spring temperature was 149 degrees, with only forty grains of salts per gallon. The only hot springs warmer than Granite and Palm (besides Penyugal) at the time were in Germany.

Steam caves were developed for spa use beneath the 1939 hotel and were accessed by elevators. Travelers through Waterman Canyon today can still see steam rising from the creek area. These steam vents are sometimes referred to as "Indian steam caves." Years ago, an attempt was made to bulldoze those caves for safety, although nature has subsequently provided a way for them to vent.

Arrowhead Springs also has fresh coldwater springs, which are quite pure, and those who came to the spa would take the sweet-tasting water home in bottles. They claimed it had curative powers. Such was the beginning of the Arrowhead Springs Water Company.

The canyon has been the victim of numerous fires and floods over the years. These floods led to the construction of the High Gear Highway in the late 1920s, which was built halfway up the side of the western canyon wall along the approximate route of Highway 18 today. This was a way to guarantee that traffic would not be hindered by the massive destruction previous floods had caused over the years, closing the canyon floor roadway.

The most recent large flood in the canyon was after the 2003 Old Fire, which stripped the south face of the mountain of all vegetation. The burned chaparral, debris and soil was washed off the hillside and down the mountain face and squeezed between the steep canyon walls during an intense rainstorm on December 25, 2003. This resulted in the deaths of fifteen persons, who were washed away by the torrents of water while they were staying at Camp Sophia (located on the creek, halfway up the canyon) for the holiday weekend.

II
LOGGERS AND SAWMILLS

DAVID SEELY COMES TO CALIFORNIA—TWICE

Historically, the name Seely/Seeley has been attached to several areas of the San Bernardino Mountains. There is Seely Flat (now Valley of Enchantment), Seely Flat Road (now Highway 138), Seeley Lane, Seeley Creek and Camp Seeley. Who was this Seeley/Seely guy, and why do people keep misspelling his name?

David Seely was born in Canada on October 12, 1819, and moved to the United States at the age of eighteen, along with his parents and brother, Wellington. He worked in the freight business on Iowa's rivers and led a colorful life as a pilot of barges on the Mississippi River, marrying Mary in 1846 and eventually moving westward with other Mormons to Salt Lake City.

Seely made his first trip to California in 1849. During the journey, his wagon train met up with the nine members of a group that, unfortunately, went on to Death Valley, where they perished. The area was named Death Valley after their ill-fated trip.

David Seely saw the San Bernardino Valley for the first time early in 1850 while traveling to board a ship at the docks at San Pedro on his way to Northern Californian to do some gold prospecting. When his ship docked in San Francisco, he was notified by Mormon leaders to return to Salt Lake City to lead a wagon train of settlers to begin a new colony in Southern California. During his travels, California became a state on September 9, 1850.

Brigham Young sent five hundred Mormon colonists to California to start the colony. Its purpose was to be an outfitting post for overseas missions for the Church of Jesus Christ of the Latter-Day Saints. The large, oxen-drawn wagon train was broken down into three smaller groups to travel to California. Because of his experience and previous travels, Captain David Seely became the leader of the second wagon train. Captain Andrew Lytle and Captain Jefferson Hunt led the other two groups. Each left Salt Lake City and traveled about one week apart so the resources along the way would not be overstressed.

The entire colony and all three parts of the wagon train were under the direction of Amasa Lyman and Charles Rich. The wagon train arrived in Sycamore Grove, near the Cajon Pass, in March 1851. Rich and Lyman purchased the Lugo Ranchero in the San Bernardino Valley on June 20, 1851, for the establishment of the colony.

San Bernardino County separated from Los Angeles County on April 26, 1853. That same year, members of the Mormon colony constructed the Mormon Lumber Road up the south face of the mountain. The purpose of the Mormon Road was to access the timber the colonists could see along

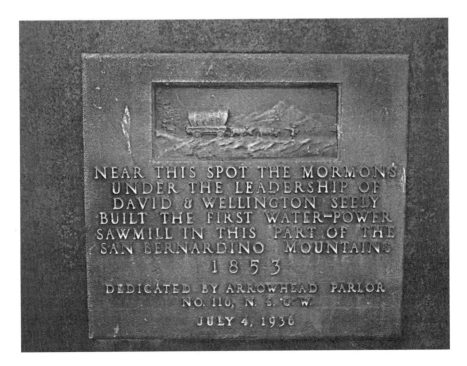

The Seely monument plaque was dedicated in 1936.

18

the mountain ridge, to which they referred as the Sierra Nevadas. The road led directly to the crest and then down into a valley, soon named Seely Flat, where David and his brother, Wellington, built the first water-powered sawmill in the San Bernardino Mountains.

Seely Creek powered the mill, and the area around the mill was called Seely Flat. The road leading to the valley from the crest soon became known as Seely Flat Road. The Seely Mill was built at the lower north end of the flat, in a meadow where Indians had lived for hundreds of years.

FIRST WATER-POWERED SAWMILL IN THE MOUNTAINS

The Seely Flat area was chosen for a full-scale lumber mill because it was predominantly covered with sugar pines and cedar trees. Sugar pine logs were the most desirable and sold for eighty dollars per thousand feet, delivered. Sugar pine is a soft, white wood without much pitch that is straight-grained and used for finish carpentry. The cedar trees were also free from pitch and were used for fence posts and wood shingles for homes. The Mormon colony in San Bernardino needed to make money to pay the Lugo family for the land it had purchased from them, and the growing community of Los Angeles needed all the lumber it could get, as it was experiencing a building boom. The Seely Brothers sawmill proved to be quite successful, despite the heavy snows that fell during the winter months and the difficulties in getting the wood down to the valley. The mill could only operate about eight months of the year, allowing the lumbermen to also farm their land in the valley and live with their families during the winter.

In the early years, Wellington and David Seely cut only medium-sized cedar and sugar pine trees, as small trees would not yield enough lumber for the effort. Trees were felled by two-man whipsaws. The very large trees were too difficult to handle without machinery, so they were left standing. The oxen then hauled the felled trees to the mill site to be cut into lumber.

The water powering the mill came from Seely Creek, carried by flume to a log cabin–type penstock about fifty feet tall. A gate at the bottom was opened to a ten-foot-diameter, undershot water-wheel that operated the vertical muley saw.

Seely's mill could process about 2,500 board feet of lumber per day. It operated day and night, from spring thaw until the water in the creek dried up to a trickle each fall. In 1854, the drought was so bad that Seely Creek totally dried up mid-summer, causing the mill to close early. This encouraged

19

This restored Mormon lumber wagon is now located in Twin Peaks.

other sawmills over on James Flat or Huston Flat to use steam power to operate their mills.

The lumber was then hauled to San Bernardino, down the Mormon Road and through West Twin Creek (Waterman) Canyon. The road was so steep in some spots (up to a 41 percent grade) that the teamsters (those who drove the wagons) would drag a log on the ground behind the wagon. This was done to prevent the heavily laden wagons from rolling over the oxen pulling the load downhill.

In June 1855, the Mormon Church, the legal authority in San Bernardino at the time, censured David Seely. Seely had hit a Jewish merchant with a piece of wood in a conflict and nearly killed the merchant. The Jewish-owned sawmill was just upstream on Seely Creek from the Seely Sawmill, and Seely, who didn't think he was getting enough water to power his mill, accused the upstream mill of slowing down or diverting his source of power. It was said that the conflict was not based on religious issues.

This was one of very few conflicts reported between mill owners and workers in the area. At one time, the Seely Flat area had up to seven sawmills, cutting different types of trees. Seely strongly disagreed with the censure.

THE FLOODED MILL

David Seely was a significant leader in the San Bernardino colony, donating a portion of the profits from his lumber mill to the Mormon Church to help pay for the purchase of the land for the Mormon colony. He was on the San Bernardino County Board of Commissioners, which helped create San Bernardino County by separating it from Los Angeles County. He became San Bernardino County's treasurer in 1853 and set the date for the election of the board of supervisors for April 13, 1854.

The next year, Seely was censured for a fight he had over water rights with an upstream sawmill. He was disappointed with the 1855 public censure and subsequently lost the title of Mormon stake president after all he had done for the colony.

When Brigham Young recalled the "religiously faithful Mormon" to return to Salt Lake City to protect the Mormon settlement from a perceived

The Seely Sawmill monument in Valley of Enchantment has a circular saw blade from the 1850s.

invasion by the federal government in 1857, many Mormon sawmill owners immediately sold their land and mills (often at pennies on the dollar) and heeded the call. Wellington Seely immediately returned to Salt Lake, but David, at first, decided to stay behind to oversee the operations of their sawmill. Since the other mills were all closed, he saw a profitable situation unfolding.

David Seely eventually, but reluctantly, returned with his son to Salt Lake City; however, they arrived after the threat of conflict was resolved. He arrived with a wagon full of items to sell from California, with the intention of returning to his wife, family and business. This infuriated church leaders in Salt Lake City even more than his tardy return. The church soon kicked both Seely and his son out of Salt Lake City. By 1860, Seely was back in San Bernardino, purchasing timber tracts, operating previously Mormon-owned sawmills and becoming prosperous, and although he remained religious, he was no longer the fervent Mormon he had once been.

The Seely Sawmill was washed away during the disastrous Noachian Flood (Noachian refers to a Noah's Ark–type flood that washes away everything), which began in December 1861 and continued through February 1862. This flood also washed out most of the county's road improvements, including the Mormon Lumber Road. Seely did not rebuild in Seely Flat, as the best trees had already been cleared from there; rather, he built his new sawmills in other locations in the mountains. The second year of flooding in 1867 convinced everyone that the Mormon Road was not in a good location, causing it to be abandoned, which pleased the new canyon owner, future California governor Robert Waterman. The 1870 Daley Mountain Turnpike Road from Del Rosa replaced it. Seely, however, continued as a lumberman, operating sawmills in the mountain area.

Seely maintained his Mormon religion, but because of his conflicts with and censure by the church and his conflicts in Salt Lake City, he was not seen as a direct or any other kind

Supervisor David Seely is depicted in the 1870s.

of representative of the church. This became a positive asset for him, as he served as a member of the San Bernardino County Board of Supervisors from 1869 to 1873. David Seely is one of only three supervisors in the past 150 years to have any direct mountain connection, although he never lived full time on the mountain. At that time, he was considered one of the most mountain-connected supervisors. He was concerned about and knew more about the mountain than most any other person in San Bernardino County.

DAVID SEELY, FIRST OWNER OF RUNNING SPRINGS

The land surrounding the headwaters of City Creek (the area now known as Running Springs) was a twenty-six-thousand-acre virgin timber tract that Seely purchased. The closest lumbering access road to the valley was down the Daley Road (just west of current-day Rim of the World High School). The headwaters of City Creek flowed into the valley through a steep-walled canyon that made the area almost inaccessible, even on horseback. Seely was convinced that a road up the City Creek Canyon was necessary. He persuaded the San Bernardino County Board of Supervisors to request an engineering survey for a road up the canyon in 1878.

Fred Perris, a state roads engineer, said a wagon road would cost in excess of $20,000. Because of the numerous bridges that would be needed to cross the deep gorges, the supervisors quickly dropped the idea and did not ever intend to build a road up City Creek Canyon.

In an effort to build his sawmill and get that timber sawed and to market, in May 1890 David Seely hired his son-in-law, Thomas McFarlane, to design and build a road up the City Creek Canyon with a maximum 10 percent grade so the possibility of installing a rail line at a later date might be achieved. "Rail access would be a valuable future asset for the development of the mountains," said Seely. McFarlane began clearing the route and designed the bridges for the road.

Seely was seventy-one years old and had worked hard all his life. He was feeling his age and decided instead to sell the City Creek acreage to the Danaher Brothers in June 1890. Subsequently, they built the Highland Lumber Mill.

David Seely died peacefully at his home at Sixth and C Streets in San Bernardino on May 24, 1892, at the age of seventy-two, surrounded by his wife, Mary, four daughters and two sons. He is considered an independent-minded mountain pioneer who started the mountain lumber industry.

The name Seely was misspelled on documents in 1914, when Los Angeles purchased land for Camp Seeley in the Seely Flats area. This mistaken spelling has become the accepted usage on maps and legal documents and is seen on such places as Seeley Way, Seeley Flat Road (aka Highway 138) and, of course, Camp Seeley. It is sad that such a significant pioneer and politician of San Bernardino County had his name misspelled by a Los Angeles office worker. Maybe it was payback for helping San Bernardino County separate from Los Angeles County sixty years earlier.

THE FIRST MOUNTAIN SAWMILLS

After the Mormon colony purchased the San Bernardino Valley from the Lugo family, it wanted to build a fort to protect its people from the marauding desert Indians, who were stealing horses and cattle and hiding them in Horsethief Canyon, near Summit Valley. The Mormons saw the trees on the ridges of the mountains above them and decided to cut them for the fort in 1851.

They also needed cash to pay for the land they had just bought for their colony and intended to sell any extra lumber they cut to raise the needed funds. The city of Los Angeles was growing quickly, and the Mormons saw a way to raise a lot of money by selling lumber to the expanding city. Over seven hundred buildings in Los Angeles were built between 1854 and 1856 with wood from the Mormon sawmills.

Charles Crismon built the first sawmill, in 1852, in West Twin Creek Canyon (Waterman Canyon). Crismon's Mill was built before the Mormon Lumber Road was constructed, and it provided the colony with much-needed fuel wood (not lumber, since it was below the pine tree level). This steam-powered mill was moved the next year to Huston Flats under present-day Lake Gregory. The first mill built on the mountaintop was the water-powered Seely Mill, constructed in 1853 and owned by brothers David and Wellington Seely (in Valley of Enchantment).

Many sawmills were portable and used steam power to turn their circular saw blades, although even the steam-powered mills still needed to be located near streams. The most common engine used was a Dolbeer engine, which supplied the power to cut the trees into boards and shingles. The portable engines and milling equipment were resold to various mill operators almost yearly and then would be hauled by oxen to a new uncut or more productive area of the forest.

Loggers and Sawmills

During the Mormon years, only medium-sized cedar and sugar pine trees were cut, as all work was hand done using two-man whipsaws to fell the trees and then hauling the trees to the mill by oxen to be cut into lumber. Small trees would not yield enough lumber for the effort, and very large trees were too difficult to handle.

The milled lumber was then transported down to San Bernardino by way of the Mormon Lumber Road, through West Twin Creek Canyon (which was so steep that some spots had a 41 percent grade), so they needed to drag a log on the ground behind the wagon to slow it down. This prevented the heavily ladened wagon from rolling over the oxen pulling the load downhill. It was a very dangerous road. When Brigham Young recalled the Mormon colonists to Utah in 1857, many sold their sawmills for pennies on the dollar or totally abandoned them to those who stayed behind.

The logging in the future Crestline area continued to grow and expand near the top of the Mormon Road in Valley of the Moon, Huston Flat, Valley of Enchantment, Cedarpines Park and other areas.

The Mormon Road was totally washed out by the 1862 Noachian Flood, and that steep route through Twin Creek Canyon was totally abandoned after flooding again in 1867. A wider and less steep lumber road was cut, up Devil's Canyon to the west to present-day Cedarpines Park, providing easy access to the Crestline area around 1870.

The James Sawmill employed a teacher for the loggers' children, and that was the first documented school in Crestline in 1853. The school and mill were moved to the Little Bear Valley area the next year.

William LaPraix, a French Canadian who wore a Van Dyke beard, had worked at the Boron Sawmill in Sawpit Canyon. He and Joseph B. Tyler decided to team up and build a new mill in June 1879 on Seely Flats. They bought and moved seventy thousand pounds of steam boilers and sawmill machinery to the new site, through Devil's Canyon, from the Excelsior Mill. They hauled the equipment with oxen and horses, taking many trips and several days to move all the gear. On one leg of the moving, one of the loaded wagons overturned, nearly killing the team.

The Tyler-LaPraix Mill was built upstream from the washed-out Seely Mill in a grove of cedar trees. LaPraix planted apple trees in the meadow next to the mill. They built flumes, boiler walls and a blacksmith shop and laid some ties for rails for cart tracks into the woods. On July 26, they blew the whistle and began sawing. Families of the lumbermen moved up for the summer, and they used the newly widened Devil's Canyon Road to transport their lumber down the mountain.

Crestline's first school monument.

The Guernsey Sawmill and lumber stacks in Crestline, circa 1900.

Loggers and Sawmills

Other sawmills in the Seely Flats area in the 1870s and '80s, besides the Tyler-LaPraix (Cedar Flats) Mill, were the Salamander Mill, Van Slyke's Mill (which became the Somer's Clipper Mill) and Anton Scherman's shingle and box mill (on Shingle Mill Creek). Despite the many mills in a small area, there is only one account of strife between them, when David Seely lost his temper. The demand was such that all could operate at full capacity and sell everything they could produce.

Beginning during the summers of the 1880s, vacationers began coming up to camp in the mountain meadows as an escape from the hot valley summers. The Seely Meadow, Huston Meadow, Dart Canyon and Devil's Canyon areas became popular locations for these "summer tent cities," close to the Devil's Canyon Road. After the Arrowhead Reservoir Toll Road opened through Waterman Canyon in the 1890s, even more vacationers arrived, using the newer road and camping at the crest and Skyland areas.

July Fourth holidays were always a big event during the sawmill era. Picnics, barbecues, log-sawing contests and other events brought the workers and their families of the various sawmills together. John Adams's 1940s July Fourth parties and barbecues in Valley of Enchantment, which eventually led to Mountaineer and Jamboree Days, can be indirectly traced back to these early-day celebrations.

The best-documented and detailed information on this sawmill era is in *The Saga of the San Bernardinos* by noted historian (and my friend) Pauliena LaFuze. Included is the entire 1880s diary of sawmill owner Joseph Tyler, detailing day-to-day activities of the sawmills in the San Bernardino mountaintop area.

It was 1893 when President Benjamin Harrison declared the creation of the 737,280-acre San Bernardino National Forest Preserve. This was to protect the watershed from being destroyed by cutting in the forest. Some of the privately owned timber tracts were still being logged, but most of the free, independent cutting was halted by this action.

Some owned and leased timber tracts continued to be sold and selectively cut through the 1920s. Redlands citrus grower Arthur Gregory, who bought his timberlands from the Arrowhead Reservoir Company in the early 1920s, continued to cut lumber through the 1930s from his privately owned lands in Valley of the Moon and Huston Flat for citrus packing boxes in Redlands. He even used the trees he cut from his land during the construction of Lake Gregory.

It is these privately owned timber tracts from which the mountain towns were developed. After the timber was consumed for commercial purposes, the land was sold to developers who began to draw up plans for vacation resorts, camping areas and vacation cabins. Today's maps reflect the limits of the National Forest from the straight lines drawn in the 1860s for those old 160-acre logging tracts.

HUSTON FLAT

Huston Flat was also known as James Flat, named for the first lumberman in that area. James moved his lumber mill to the Little Bear Valley area after finishing the first cut in the vicinity. James was also the first man to hire a teacher for his children, initiating education in the mountains.

Daniel Huston began working in 1855 as a lumberman in the area and helped rebuild the Salamander Mill after it was destroyed by fire in 1859. The area soon became known as Huston Flat, and the creek nearby was called Huston Creek (sometimes misspelled by the county as Houston). Huston continued to operate sawmills in the mountain area until forced to quit in 1875 because of serious injuries he suffered from the claws and teeth of a grizzly bear. Huston Flat was flooded when the dam at Lake Gregory was completed in 1938. Huston Creek is now the route of water exiting from the spillway of Lake Gregory, sending the water on its way down to Silverwood Lake.

III

FOREST VACATIONERS AND
HOMESTEADERS

BYRON WATERS

Prominent attorney and California assemblyman of San Bernardino County
Byron Waters homesteaded the Seely Flats area of Crestline at the turn
of the twentieth century, as the sawmills were leaving the area. Seely Flats
was named for former county supervisor David Seely, who started the first
sawmill in the area in the 1850s. Byron had been in the San Bernardino area
since he was eighteen years old, in 1867.

Waters was born in 1849 in Cherokee County, Georgia. His family's farm
was in the line of Sherman's March to the Sea during the Civil War and
had been looted to the ground. To understand why Waters would move to
California, you must understand a little about his uncle, James (Jim) Waters.

James Waters was a noted mountain man, trapper and hunter who hung
out with Kit Carson, "Old Bill" Williams and John Brown from the 1830s to
the 1850s. Waters had numerous narrow escapes from death at the hands of
Indians and suffered serious injuries.

After the decline of the fur trade, Jim Waters became a guide for pack trains
from St. Louis to Southern California along the Old Spanish Trail through
the Mojave Desert and Cajon Pass. That route, although more of a year-
round trail, was a more dangerous way to get to California than the Sierra
Nevada route because of unpredictable Indians and unreliable water sources.

James's friend John Brown had converted to the Mormon faith and
convinced Waters to move to the San Bernardino colony, where Brown had
lived for three years and had become the justice of the peace.

Waters arrived in San Bernardino in 1856, settling first in Yucaipa. Waters was reunited with many of his mountain men friends in the colony and stayed. When Brigham Young recalled the Mormon faithful to return to Salt Lake City in 1857, many elected public offices became vacant, as the "saints" dropped everything and sold their lands to leave quickly. Waters ran in the election of 1858 for public administrator and won. He was elected to the board of supervisors' Third District in 1863 and the Second District in 1865, serving until 1869. He was elected again in 1874 and 1877, becoming chairman of the board of supervisors in 1879 and again in 1880.

James Waters helped start the first legitimate theater in Southern California. In 1882, he and his partners built the two-story San Bernardino Opera House at D Street and Court Street.

James Waters easily convinced his eighteen-year-old nephew to move to San Bernardino in 1867 after the destruction of Byron's father's farm during the Civil War. James at that time had his farm in Yucaipa and was a county supervisor. There was much to entice young Byron to join his successful uncle in California and not much keeping him in Georgia.

Byron told the following story about his uncle James putting his "mountain man" knowledge to good use after the flood of 1867:

> *Uncle Jim was out on a trip of inspection of the roads, and on reaching the site of the former ford of the Santa Ana River, found a concourse of people, some on horseback, and some in wagons of various descriptions. None seemed inclined to test the crossing, although they had cut an approach through the bluff bank. Uncle Jim inquired why they were waiting. What you have to do is break a road and settle the ground, I'll show you. He insisted the horsemen follow him and they rode back and forth through the river and did encounter some patches of quicksand, but they rode back and forth until the quick sand was settled and after that all the vehicles and wagons were able to cross in safety.*

Byron, soon after his arrival in California, decided to enter the study of law in 1869 under the offices of Judge H.C. Rolfe, and later Judge H.M. Willis, and was admitted to the bar in 1871.

Waters was said to be a fiery, brusque and somewhat arrogant attorney, always ready for a legal fight. One case from early in his career that was recounted by Judge Rolfe began when Byron was annoyed and angered when a judge admitted evidence that Waters thought was inappropriate and incriminating against his client. Despite much legal arguing, he could not seem to change the judge's mind. Waters abruptly walked out of the courtroom and went to a Superior Court judge nearby, arguing that he order the evidence removed from the case.

That judge reminded Waters that the other judge's decision could be appealed when the case was decided. Dejected, Waters returned to his courtroom to find it empty. In his absence, the judge had sent the case to the jury.

Despite the evidence, his client was found not guilty. Waters had won the case. No one knows if his courtroom theatrics influenced or hindered his client's case, but he did get some publicity.

The first time Waters's name was mentioned in relation to the mountains was in 1870, after Edward Daley had built his relatively safe ten- to fifteen-degree-grade "Mountain Turnpike" wagon road from Del Rosa to Little Bear Valley (Lake Arrowhead) with "axes, scrapers and dynamite." (The Daley Mountain Turnpike road crossed the crest of the mountain just east of Rimforest. An oxen yoke monument marks the site.)

The Bear Springs sawmill men invited everyone up the mountain for a Fourth of July barbecue in the "coolness of the heights" to celebrate the opening of the road. For that official Fourth of July celebration and dedication of the new road, one of the guest speakers was "young lawyer Byron Waters," who made "short, but impressive remarks."

Byron Waters did many things to make his name known locally. Since his uncle James had been a well-known mountain man, Byron's natural interest was in preserving the mountain environment. He filed numerous lawsuits demanding the preservation of the natural environment.

In 1877, Waters was elected to the California General Assembly, representing San Bernardino County, during the same election in which his uncle won another term on the county board of supervisors. Byron was becoming recognized as one of the Democratic leaders of the area, so much that he was appointed a delegate-at-large for the California Constitutional Convention and assisted in the writing of the new state constitution.

In 1881, Byron Waters organized the second bank in San Bernardino County, the Farmers Exchange Bank, and served as its president until 1884. He then went back to practicing law and was credited as one of the ablest lawyers in the state. Waters was considered a lawyer of "unusual acumen and good judgment" as he matured. He took several young men into his law firm to train them. One of them, newly admitted lawyer James A. Gibson, worked with Waters until he was elected to the Superior Court in 1884.

In 1888, Waters was on the board of directors with the Chino Valley Manufacturing Company. The iron-rolling plant was to use the iron

Byron Waters was a homesteader of Seely Flats in 1900.

discovered at Daggett, but the financial boom collapsed, and the plant went under. By 1889, Assemblyman Waters had built a large house in the affluent Bunker Hill area of San Bernardino. On the west base of that hill was the crumbling adobe home of Vicente Lugo, the son of Antonio Maria Lugo, who sold the San Bernardino Rancho to Lyman and Rich for the Mormon colony in 1851, just thirty-eight years before. When the mountains opened up to homesteading at the turn of the twentieth century, Byron Waters took advantage of the offer. He grew apples on his homesteaded Seely Flats land. Some of those apple trees had been planted by the mountain's own "Johnny Appleseed," lumberman LaPraix, and other sawmill workers at the numerous lumber mills that had been in the area since the Seely brothers built the first sawmill on Seely Creek in the 1850s.

Byron Waters ran in August 1900 for the nomination of Superior Court judge but lost in a three-way tie and then continued his law practice. Waters began to go blind in the late 1910s. He began to divide his land in 1923. He was now seventy-three years old. Waters sold Frank A. Tetley Sr. from Riverside more than half the land from his 1900s homestead in 1924, and Tetley developed the Rim of the World Park, which has become known today as Valley of Enchantment. Tetley named the main street "Waters Drive" in recognition of Waters's many accomplishments in San Bernardino County. (So, despite the water that was always flowing over the roadway after a storm, the road is not named Waters Drive for that flowing creek water, as I always believed as a child.)

Waters loved the fresh, cool mountain air and water and his mountain home and having his son, Byron Waters Jr., drive him up the mountain, experiencing the thrill of riding to the mountains on the paved High Gear Road after it was finished in 1933. That was quite a contrast from the bumpy wagon ride he had taken sixty-three years earlier, going up the Daley

Canyon Road in 1870 for that July Fourth celebrating the opening of the Daley Mountain Turnpike Road.

Byron Waters died in 1935 at eighty-six years of age during the era of telephones, electricity, automobiles and mountain subdivisions. Byron Waters was a self-made man who helped initiate great changes in the world around him.

In the 1950s, the private Club San Moritz purchased the remaining Byron Waters land in Valley of Enchantment from the family and used it to build the club's Pitch and Putt Golf Course for its members. The golf area became a popular venue among Club San Moritz members, their kids and guests. The former driveway that accessed that land from Highway 138 was named Byron Road.

When Club San Moritz closed in the mid-1970s, the land was sold. That acreage next to Valley of Enchantment Elementary School was laid out as an upscale mobile home park with a clubhouse on the hill for its residents. Those who live on Byron Road or Waters Drive should take pride in living on streets named after such a significant man in mountain and San Bernardino County history.

THE STORY OF SKYLAND

Forgotten Skyland, Crestline's Original Tract

The mountain area known as Skyland is located just east of Old Town Crestline, on the south side of Skyland Peak and Crest Forest Drive. People first came to camp at Skyland during the sawmill days in the 1870s because of its beauty. The views were fantastic since Skyland faces San Bernardino Valley with an excellent view all the way to the Pacific Ocean. Catalina Island could be seen on a clear day, and the air was cool and clean. It was not an area that was extensively logged, as even the lumbermen—including Little Bear Valley sawmill owner Joe Tyler—appreciated its uniqueness and location and built cabins there overlooking the valley. It was a perfectly situated summer campground under the tall trees.

The entire mountaintop area at that time was considered "Pineland." It was 1895 when a group of forty Colton residents came in horse-drawn wagons up the newly opened Arrowhead Reservoir Toll Road to a place they called Camp Indolence to escape the blistering summer heat. It was an arduous six-hour wagon trek just to reach the crest, and it was necessary to bring all the needed camping supplies and food. Mr. Sprecher set up Camp Indolence on the Skyland Cliff front near the Ferncliff cottage of architect T.H. Goff. The area was near the Guernsey Sawmill and the apple orchards behind Skyland Peak. Campers would go out on excursions to the orchards, fishing streams, sawmills and meadows from the campgrounds. Skyland developed as a public campground area around the same time as the private Squirrel Inn Resort, just a mile up Crest Road, beyond Horseshoe Bend.

It was during this 1890s "conservation of nature era," as the National Forest Preserve was first created, that John Andreson Sr. (pronounced ann-Drey-sen) first brought his family to the mountains to camp, and they learned to appreciate our area. The father and son would both become San Bernardino County supervisors and make a lasting impression on the future Crestline area, each authorizing better roads to access the mountains.

By 1902, an observation deck was built at the camp, on the cliff, to view the valley below and the heavens above. On many summer evenings, the campers at Skyland would build a large bonfire that could be seen from the valley below, as far away as Grand Terrace. What an excellent, almost free, advertising gimmick—the bonfire seemed to brag to the sweltering valley residents about the cool, mountain resort within sight of their homes. Surely that bonfire encouraged many to make the difficult daylong journey by horse and buggy up the steep logging roads to the resort. They called it Skyland because visitors felt heavenly inspired, like they could almost reach out and touch the stars and planets.

W.M. Pierson from Riverside built the Skyland Inn in 1903. The Skyland Inn was, at the time, the first stop for the horse-drawn stages that brought visitors to the mountains. It had a gramophone in the parlor for entertainment. The cook used local fresh produce from the gardens and dairy. The local homesteaders in the area, such as the Knapp family (Knapp's Cutoff), would sell fresh fruits such as apples, milk and vegetables to the campers. The inn had eighteen guests registered that first week in June and many more families camped in the campground.

Outside activities included horseshoes and croquet, along with horseback riding, hiking, fishing in local streams and relaxing in the cool mountain air. Evening activities started with watching the breathtaking sunsets, followed by watching the flickering electric lights come on in the valley below. William Stephens (lovingly called "Uncle Billy") would visit and entertain with his concertina, or local forest ranger Easton would play the violin. Many campers rented the "furnished" tent cabins at the camp, which had cots so you were not sleeping on the ground, and they could enjoy the entertainment at the inn. Beginning in 1904, several more privately owned cottages were built in the Skyland area. The Andreson family, which had two county supervisors in their family over the years, returned to stay at Skyland for many years.

The county purchased the Arrowhead Toll Road in 1905, and in 1906, it became a free county road, doubling the traffic up the road, and business at the resorts really picked up, filling the various camps all through the summer season. It now took "only" four hours for a four-horse wagon to make it to the summit, where the Skyland was the first resort stop for the Mountain Stage Line. Skyland Camp added a new pavilion, where there were dances and songfests, and often eighty persons would be involved in a whist (card game) tournament. Two hundred guests attended the end-of-the-season party.

In December 1905, the Arrowhead Reservoir and Power Company, since it no longer had exclusive use of the old toll road, announced that an incline cable car system was being built to bring the bags of cement up the face of the mountain to Skyland for the dam the company was building in Little Bear Valley (this dam created Lake Arrowhead). Called "the Incline," it was completed in the summer of 1906. It didn't work too well; however, in December 1906, it did safely transport the Vredenborg family down the mountain quickly when their baby became extremely ill. While rapidly descending the mountain, the mother-in-law became scared and jumped out of the cable car. It stopped, she got back in (only slightly injured) and they safely continued the trip to the hospital.

Skyland Heights Becomes a Popular Resort, 1905–1911

The first post office on the mountain (west of Fredalba) was opened in the Skyland Inn by John Hansen in June 1907. He named the post office "Incline" because of its location near the upper terminus of the Incline Railroad cable car system. It was anticipated that the Incline Railroad would attract a lot of tourists who would like to ride it up the mountain instead of making the long six- to eight-hour trek by wagon up the Arrowhead Reservoir Road.

In attracting vacationers, there was a lot of friendly competition between the fashionable, although exclusive, Squirrel Inn and the Skyland Inn. Skyland scheduled balls and musicals (and Uncle Billy with his concertina) and regularly had 150 guests between the inn and the campground. Visitors could relax, playing billiards, horseshoes or croquet, hiking and listening to the windup phonograph, as there was no electricity on the mountaintop. Sitting in a picture-frame tree was one of the must-do activities while visiting

This picture-frame tree
was in Skyland.

Skyland. The Emerick family opened the Valley View Grocery for the convenience of those camping.

In 1907, the two-year-old pavilion at Skyland burned down, toasting the piano, the campground's rental tents and camp bedding. Despite the pavilion fire, the Skyland Heights area continued to be popular.

After the Incline fell into disuse because it didn't work well, in 1910, new postmaster Jeremiah Hattery changed the post office's name to Skyland Heights.

The Skyland Inn and Camp had its own water supply, stables and produce. Food and staples were available at the Skyland General Store, which was in the same building as the Skyland Resort's office. The Skyland Inn charged $2.50 a day for lodging and food. Even hot or cold baths were available.

Then, on Tuesday, July 25, 1911, at 1:00 p.m., in more than one-hundred-degree heat, a fire began in Waterman Canyon. Hot summer winds caught the flames and swept them up through the thick mountainside chaparral.

It crossed the Crest Road (now called Crest Forest Drive) in several locations, threatening Skyland.

The vacationers in Skyland safely escaped to Little Bear Meadow. The fire grew to three miles wide and one mile long across the mountain's southern front.

Suddenly, at 3:00 p.m. on Sunday, amid new wind, ash and smoke, the fire again began to attack Skyland. Some of the outer tent cabins were destroyed, but the hardworking firefighters saved the inn, cabins and the Incline Railroad tracks.

By 3:30 a.m. on Monday, July 31, winds were still

The Incline rail tracks in 1907.

whipping the flames; they were leaping up to two hundred feet high in the sky but stayed below the Crest Road. The fire had been burning for seven days, and the firefighters were exhausted from the scorching temperatures they endured while fighting the fire and making firebreaks with hand shovels. Wherever possible, they fought the fire with water from fire trucks, as motorized vehicles had just been allowed to drive on mountain roads that year.

Then, on Tuesday, August 1, sudden gusts of wind blew the fire quickly up to the Skyland Crest, and the Incline Railroad track and trestles were destroyed. Both Clifton Heights and Skyland were ablaze. The Skyland Inn was saved but singed. Three private cabins were totally destroyed.

Finally, by Sunday, August 6, thirteen days after it started, the fire was finally under control. Over 12,900 acres had been burned. The total cost for suppressing the fire was about $17,000 for labor and supplies. The value of the Incline Railroad and the buildings destroyed was not included in that figure. Skyland suffered burned cabins, houses, tents and trees, as well as the loss of the Incline Railroad.

Where Movie Stars Leo Maloney and Bela Lugosi Lived

The mountain area around Skyland became a popular place to shoot movies beginning in 1911, as it had good weather, bright sunlight and varied terrains; was not too far from Hollywood; and had telephone service and great lodging available at both the Skyland Inn and the Pinecrest Resort near current-day Twin Peaks.

The silent movie era brought many film companies and their famous stars to the mountains. Leo Maloney was a "winsome" western star who had his own production company, which made "off-beat" western comedies. Several of them were filmed in the Skyland area in the early 1920s.

Leo Maloney built his movie studio near his vacation home in Skyland. Maloney liked the Skyland area so much that his production company purchased several acres of the western portion of Huston Flat in 1926, spending a purported $100,000 to build a "permanent western façade town" as his movie studio. He intended to have a year-round studio with thirty-five full-time actors and crew employed. Unfortunately, he had poor timing.

The Leo D. Maloney Production Company made at least four movies there, including *The High Hand*, *Outlaw Express* and *Long Loop on the Pecos*, with two more on the schedule when the Pathe Picture Corporation (which distributed his movies) went broke after talkies took over the movie business.

At least eighteen movies were produced at the Maloney western set after the western village sets were leased out to other movie studios and production companies. Most two-reel silent movies took about two to three weeks to shoot. Several of the movies shot there, such as *Don Desperado*, starred the popular "Bullets, the Wonder Dog."

The buildings in Maloney's western town set were mostly Old West–era, false-front buildings. At the blacksmith shop building, however, they actually did shoe horses, but because the forge did not work, they brought in prefabricated horseshoes.

The set was built on the south side of where Lake Drive in Crestline is now, just east of Alder Lane. The movie town jail was situated across from where the Stockade is now. West of the jail was where Leo Maloney had the caretaker live in a small cabin. The commissary, which had a kitchen and dining area and living quarters for the crew, was built where the Crestline Post Office is located today.

A false-front barn, which stored a stagecoach and oats and hay for the horses, was at the corner where B & L Liquor is today. Next to the blacksmith shop was a harness and saddle shop, and down the path was the general

Forest Vacationers and Homesteaders

Leo Maloney's movie studio western set, which is now the center of Lake Gregory Village on Lake Drive.

store. The saloon (what Old West town would be complete without one?) was across from the general store, on the north side.

Other producers to use the Old West town were Yakima Knutte and Bob Custers, and actor Hoot Gibson shot several movies at Maloney's set. Those two-reel silent movies, like the set, are now only memories of a bygone era.

Actors and movie industry people so enjoyed the scenic and natural beauty of the Skyland area that many of them bought vacation cabins there. Horror film actor Bela Lugosi had a cabin on Venus Way in the Skyland area. Since he came to the mountains to relax, he stayed close to his cabin. He loved nature and enjoyed his fabulous Skyland-area view of the forest and the valley below.

Crestline's Oldest Vacation Area

When the Rim of the World Highway opened to personal automobile traffic in 1915, the Skyland Inn was successful in competing for guests against the new resorts that soon developed along the highway. Skyland also added more activities, such as a story hour for children.

During the early years of the twentieth century, in the days before air conditioning, people felt compelled to leave the blazing heat of the valley and came to the mountains to enjoy horseback riding, hiking, stream fishing, horseshoes and croquet and to relax in the shade of the tall pine trees, with mountain breezes at least twenty degrees cooler than those in the sizzling valley below.

The Skyland Inn's rates were fifteen dollars per person, per week, which included meals. A furnished housekeeping cabin was ten dollars per week for two, or twenty dollars per month. A tent cabin rented for seven dollars per week for two persons. The average vacationer came for two or more weeks during the late 1910s and early 1920s.

It was 1919 when S.W. Dillin, the new Skyland Heights postmaster, moved the post office away from Skyland to a building he purchased in the newly developing area of Crestline.

W.O. Raub (who also owned Strawberry Flats) purchased the five acres composing the Skyland Inn and began a renovation project. A new, direct, auto-friendlier road (meaning a gentler road grade and wider lanes), which passed next to the Skyland Inn, was completed in 1921.

Ramsay and Mann subdivided Skyland in 1923. Timing is everything, and the popularity of Skyland and many of the other older resorts, such as Fredalba and

This brochure advertised Skyland Heights.

Pinecrest, suffered with fewer visitors when the new, modern Lake Arrowhead Resort and Village opened in 1924 on the shore of Lake Arrowhead.

The Skyland Inn was upgraded and remodeled several times and continued to host vacationers until 1955, when the historic wooden inn was destroyed by fire. All that now remains of the Skyland Inn are the stone steps descending from Skyland Drive. Several other inns, mini motels and bed-and-breakfasts also operated in Skyland over the years for the same reasons the early vacationers chose the area—views, cool breezes and as a retreat from the everyday world.

The 1923 Survey Was Wrong

Skyland Camp was surveyed and subdivided into vacation cabin sites by developers Ramsay and Mann in 1923. The Skyland Forest theme emphasized the romance of the history of the Skyland area with street names like Saturn, Jupiter, Mercury, Mars, Venus, Neptune and Inspiration. Skyland Drive is a semicircular street that curves southward from Crest Forest Drive toward the crest and back to the main road.

Charles S. Mann wrote about Skyland in 1925 in his advertising brochure: "There is no sense of congestion, nor are there rows of houses visible, each being screened, to a certain extent...by the land contours and large, full trees." Skyland became the expensive section of the Crestline community. As Mann developed the rest of the town, he kept the price of the lots in Skyland more expensive due to the historically desirable location and views.

The subdivision slowly grew, one house at a time, and soon the Crestline school bus was driving along Skyland Drive, picking up students attending the Crest Forest School, which opened in 1929. The area became an upscale residential section of Crestline. As the years progressed, the original homes became older, and as new sections of the community were developed with larger homes, Skyland's desirability lessened.

In 1980, the Panorama Fire licked the Skyland area and caused all the residents to evacuate as the fire threatened to jump Highway 18 and burn the area like it did in 1911. After the fire, the National Forest wanted to verify its borders along the highway.

In December 1982, after many years of Skyland being a quiet residential alcove off the beaten path, the government re-survey of National Forest land discovered that the original 1923 survey was in error. Seventeen homeowners had unknowingly bought and built on National Forest land, and the conflict was on.

Respected citizen David Press, judge of the Crest Forest Justice Court, was one of those seventeen. He was shocked when he was notified that half his house was on government property, especially since there were homes on all four sides of him. In fact, the line went directly through the middle of his living room.

Lawsuits ensued when the government wanted the homeowners to tear down their homes, some over fifty years old. This put all seventeen homeowners in the position of not having clear and conveyable titles to their homes. The story hit newspapers and TV for several years after the homeowners were interviewed.

When all the legal entanglements were finally settled in 1984, the homes were allowed to stay, but the government demanded and was paid for the encroachment on its land at the Forest Service exchange price of $2,000 an acre. No one was happy with the settlement, but they were relieved the conflict was finally over.

Fortunately, only two property owners, the Millers and Morans, had to pay for more than half an acre, and all homeowners were prorated on the percentage of an acre of their unintentional encroachment. Judge Press paid the additional $186 to keep his house and clear the title to his land. This resulted in strange ownership deeds to the property, with most of the homes now having two deeds attached to each property and two property tax bills each year, unless the property owner paid additional money to the county for a lot consolidation.

The 2003 Old Fire did more than lick the Skyland area. The fire raced up Waterman Canyon to Skyland Peak, destroying thirty-three homes on the east end of Skyland during the first twenty-four hours of the seven-day-long fire. Those homes destroyed were in a densely treed area on the south side of Skyland Drive with very narrow one-car-wide streets that fire engines could not safely enter. The fire engines made their stand on Skyland Drive. The fire jumped Skyland in one spot, singeing three more homes. Since the fire, the area has been cleared of all the burned homes and trees, and despite the construction of about ten homes in the area, it is still devoid of most greenery ten years after the fire. Many residents learned of their lost homes through TV coverage of the fire, but because most of the reporters couldn't figure out the names of the various communities, mislabeling most of them, uncertainty reigned until they returned three weeks later.

Skyland is the original developed area of Crestline, with a long and colorful history, but most mountain residents have nearly forgotten its location and significance today.

DR. WESLEY THOMPSON

A name not familiar to most mountain residents today but very familiar to residents of San Bernardino County over one hundred years ago is that of Dr. Wesley Thompson. He achieved significant recognition in his lifetime, and he also left a lasting impression on the Crestline area.

Wesley Thompson was born on June 30, 1845, in Fort Wayne, Indiana, the son of an Indiana pioneer. His early education took place in a log schoolhouse and then he attended M.E. Seminary in Tippecanoe. He finished his education at Asbury, now known as Des Plaines University.

Thompson joined the Eighty-seventh Regiment of the U.S. Army, a part of the Indiana Army Corps Volunteers, in 1863 during the Civil War. He was under General Sherman in the Atlantic Campaign and marched with the general during the historic March to the Sea. It was unknown to him at the time, but the army destroyed a farm belonging to the parents of Byron Waters, another man who was significant in San Bernardino Mountain history. Thompson was with the army during the surrender of General Johnson and during the grand review in Washington, D.C. He was discharged from the army in Louisville, Kentucky, after two years of service at the age of twenty.

Thompson returned to Indiana in 1865 and entered the pharmaceutical drug business; he then began attending medical school at Reasling. He finished his education at Miami Medical College in Cleveland, Ohio, in 1869. Thompson practiced medicine in Effingham, Illinois, for eighteen years. During those years, he married Mary M. Little, who developed poor health. Doctors determined that a move to the dry, warm California climate would benefit Mary.

In 1887, the family moved to Del Rosa, north and east of San Bernardino, California, where Dr. Thompson opened a new medical practice. Wesley and Mary were the parents of six children: Victor, Mary, Rubie, Jennie, Ada and Emma.

It was only two years later, in 1889, that his medical expertise was noted, and he was elected coroner of San Bernardino County. He served at least three four-year terms in that position, while continuing his medical practice. He was actively involved in the Del Rosa School District and was elected to the school board.

The Thompson family enjoyed coming to the San Bernardino Mountains for vacations, to escape the summer heat of the San Bernardino Valley. The family used both the Arrowhead Reservoir Toll Road and the Daley Canyon

Andy Fletcher Triangle Park, where Fly Camp began prior to 1906.

Road (which went directly from Del Rosa to the Little Bear area) to reach the summit. However, Thompson preferred the Arrowhead Toll Road, as it was less steep and wider, and there were fewer out-of-control lumber wagons going down that road than on the steeper and narrower Daley Road. One of the areas he frequented was the campground at Skyland. He could look down from the summit and see his own home from there. He often camped near the crest in an area referred to as "Fly Camp." It got its name because the Arrowhead Reservoir Company had its horse and oxen corrals nearby at the crest of the toll road.

In 1906, lumberman Henry Guernsey was trying to develop 630 acres of his harvested timber tract land located north of Skyland into a summertime recreational destination. There was a great desire of valley residents to escape the one-hundred-plus-degree temperatures of the valley and enjoy the fishing and camping under the tall pines. Guernsey dug wells so visitors would have easy access to water, and he cleared the underbrush. The county had just opened the former Arrowhead Reservoir Toll Road to free public usage. Guernsey held a contest for naming his new Crest Resort. There were 180 name submissions in the contest, one of which was "Summer City in the Pines."

However, the winning name suggestion came from none other than the county's coroner, Dr. Wesley Thompson, who suggested the short, technically correct and catchy name of Crestline. He won a lot suitable for building a cabin in Crestline, one of the first vacation developments on the mountain. Guernsey began building Thompson's cabin and one for himself in his new tract as soon as the contest was concluded. By 1908, there were fourteen cabins in the tract, as well as the Crest Corner Market and a general merchandise market on the main road to Lake Arrowhead. Dr. Thompson was elected to another four-year term as county coroner after winning the contest. However, the name and success of the subdivision were both short-lived but not totally forgotten.

It was in 1919 that postmaster Samuel W. Dillin (De-Lynn) moved the Skyland Heights Post Office down from the snowy elevation of Skyland into his new grocery and photography store and stage stop nearby (current corner of Crest Forest Drive and Highway 138). Dillin chose the common usage name of Crestline to identify the area. When the post office received the name of Crestline, Dr. Thompson's winning name again had significance.

Dr. Thompson and family were there to witness the beginnings of Crestline as a real community as the 1915 Rim of the World Road went straight through what eventually became the middle of town, the route of current-day Crest Forest Drive. Subdivisions began to sprout up all over the mountains.

Dr. Wesley Thompson's naming of Crestline in 1906 may be best remembered for removing the onus of the area's previous moniker, "Fly Camp." Everyone who lives in the area today should remember and thank him for that.

CELEBRATE ONE HUNDRED YEARS OF CRESTLINE

At exactly 2:00 p.m. on July 23, 1906, it was announced that the Crest Resort Company's board of directors, which was headed by lumberman Henry Guernsey, had selected the name "Crestline" as the new name for the mountaintop area.

On July 23, 2006, to celebrate this significant point in Crestline's history, a celebration was held at the corner of Lake Gregory Drive and Lake Drive, across from Lake Gregory.

This mural on Goodwin's Market celebrated the 100th anniversary of Crestline.

A ribbon-cutting ceremony revealed a new mural that had been painted on the front wall of Goodwin's Market, facing the lake. Molly Collins's mural, *A Tribute to the California Grizzly Bear*, was revealed to mark the Centennial Celebration. Speeches were given by various members of the community honoring the creation of the mural and the anniversary of the naming of Crestline. Then the community rocked out to a live band.

The mural is a multimedia project. Collins combined large wooden sculptures of forest animals with a painted forest setting and words to create a fitting tribute to the demise of the grizzly bear, not only from the San Bernardino Mountains, but also from the state of California. The words of tribute on the mural state:

> *The Grizzly Bear, a symbol of great strength, once roamed California in great numbers. They were universally feared, for when one stood it towered twelve feet and their numbers were in excess of 10,000 or more. These great carnivores were embedded in myths and legends of Native Americans and settlers alike. Their numbers quickly declined as they were killed off by the hundreds due to civilization closing in on their habitat. In 1953, the California Legislature named the extinct California Grizzly our state animal. The Grizzly, the symbol of our state, was gone forever.*

The celebration honored the choice of the name "Crestline," submitted by former San Bernardino County coroner Dr. Wesley Thompson, to name the crest area in 1906.

Forest Vacationers and Homesteaders

The year 1906 is also significant because it is when the county opened the previously private Arrowhead Reservoir Toll Road to the public and made it into a free county wagon road, thus opening access to the mountains to everyone, leading to the development of the mountain communities.

HORSESHOE BEND

Horseshoe Bend Mountain Club Is One Hundred Years Old

The Horseshoe Bend area was called back in 1959 "the forest that time has forgotten." Bob Dubbell, a Horseshoe Bend Mountain Club property owner, described it thusly: "Its peacefulness, breathtaking panoramas, the forest, the birds, animals and the cohesiveness of the residents have made the area a jewel and an outstanding community in the San Bernardino Mountains."

But the beginning of the Horseshoe Bend Summer Tract fifty years earlier in 1909 was not the first time that the Horseshoe Bend area was identified by name in the history books. Bart Smithson attached the name Horseshoe Bend to that area of the crest region in 1891. He was contracted to build a road eastward from where the Arrowhead Reservoir Toll Road met the crest over to Little Bear Valley to move the equipment and bags of cement needed to build the dam. Above the headwaters of Huston Creek, about one and a half miles east of current-day Old Town Crestline, the road made a sharp U-turn and was referred to as the "Horseshoe Bend" by Smithson.

The first mention of Horseshoe Bend in *The Saga of the San Bernardinos* by Pauliena LaFuze was in 1895 as a reference point when Calvin Baker was setting up a sawmill. He chose a forested location that had been mostly ignored by the other mills, described as "above the Skyland Tollhouse." He planned to "cut the timber running all the way to Horseshoe Bend," and he was busy milling wood there in 1897.

In 1898, Baker's daughter, Angie, married Henry Guernsey's son, Roy. Henry Guernsey had a timber tract that extended on the north side of Skyland down the hill to current-day Crestline. Both the Baker and Guernsey mills stopped milling for the big celebration that day in May 1898. After that, both fathers worked cooperatively together, especially since their mills adjoined each other in the Skyland–Horseshoe Bend areas just below the crest.

In an 1899 article in *House Beautiful* magazine about the exclusive Squirrel Inn resort, the inn was referred to as located at Horseshoe Bend, so by this time the name had generalized to the nearly one-mile-long stretch of the mountain's crest that overlooked the valley at the time.

Around 1900, Guernsey and Baker became partners with Redlands citrus grower Arthur Gregory. Baker moved on to other timberlands away from the Horseshoe Bend area and managed other mills owned by Gregory. In 1900, the Horseshoe Bend Mill land was actually sold to Gregory and Guernsey, who continued to run the mill. Guernsey later divided his lands into a vacation cabin site in 1906 and ran a contest to name the area; the name Crestline was chosen.

The Arrowhead Reservoir Company purchased the rights to drill a tunnel under the Horseshoe Bend area to send its water to the San Bernardino Valley as part of its irrigation water project in 1901. It appeared the company was planning to send its irrigation water down through newly named Waterman Canyon to the valley below. In 1905, Frank Mooney, the nephew of Arrowhead Reservoir Company (ARC) executive James Edgar Mooney, was out surveying for the pipeline that was to go under the Horseshoe Bend area. A new road was "brushed" (the removal of the underbrush along the route planned for a dirt road) during the summer of 1906 through the Horseshoe Bend area from the Incline to Little Bear Valley.

Horseshoe Bend Summer Tract

June 1, 1909, was the beginning of the Horseshoe Bend summer tract—the first time forestland was offered for summer tract leases by the U.S. Forest Service in the San Bernardino Mountains. In 1909, most campers didn't arrive until the end of June, when the weather got warm, but the leases were signed for use from Memorial Day until Labor Day each season. Other summer tracts were established after the success of Horseshoe Bend, including one at Strawberry Flats, which opened in 1914.

The Horseshoe Bend summer tract was established along the original two-lane dusty wagon trail, initially known as the Crest Road, which was the main road until the Rim of the World Road (now Crest Forest Drive) was established in 1915, when auto traffic was permitted. That main route was replaced when the High Gear Highway was built on the south side of the mountain face below Horseshoe Bend in the latter 1920s.

The summer tract runs along three-quarters of a mile of the crest above and on the south side of Crest Forest Drive about one and a half miles east of current uptown Crestline and just west of Arrowhead Highlands, overlooking the San Bernardino Valley. Its elevation ranges from 5,130 to 5,405 feet. Now that it is off the main road, few know of its existence and even fewer about its unique history.

In the initial tract offering in 1909, there were thirteen lots developed by the Forest Service. The lease cost was fifteen dollars per year, but only summer usage was permitted. Mr. Merriam pitched the first tent in the tract in 1909. His family would come and stay for the entire summer to escape the blistering San Bernardino summer heat, arriving in a horse and wagon, bringing with them all the necessaries for the summer. Mr. Merriam would hike up the face of the mountain from work to visit them most weekends.

Merriam then built the first cabin in Horseshoe Bend in 1914. By 1917 (after the stage line and auto were allowed to drive up the Rim of the World Road beginning in 1915), there were many families staying in the summer in tents at Horseshoe Bend. The families would entertain one another while the men would go to the Pinecrest Resort to play cards in the afternoon.

The Horseshoe Bend summer tract developed in a very family-friendly manner. The Merriam family invited their friends and relatives to join in the summer mountain fun. Mr. Merriam built the first cabin in space number five in 1914. The family would come and camp all summer on their leased space.

An early summer vacationer at Horseshoe Bend was Peter J. Dubbell and his family. He was one of the first certified public accountants in

A vacationer builds a cabin in Crestline, circa 1920s.

California. He built cabin number twenty-six on lot forty-six, right at the road's horseshoe. Inside the horseshoe are the tract's playground and hiking trails. Dubbell started the yearly meetings of the Horseshoe Bend Mountain Club in 1918 and became its first secretary, succeeded by his wife, Bertha. She lived at their cabin in Horseshoe Bend until 1967. Their son, Bob, then retired to that same 1916 cabin in 1977, residing there until 1993.

The security of knowing where the family would spend their summer away from the blistering heat of the valley below and knowing who their neighbors would be made this area a retreat of immense value to those families who leased year after year. Friendships and relationships developed between the families that have lasted generations. The activities of exploring the forest, the quiet enjoyment of watching the animals, learning to trap and fish and hiking and reading were pleasures looked forward to all year long and treasured as wonderful ways to pass the summers.

Horseshoe Bend was on the main road for years. From 1910 through about 1920, the motor mail stage drove right through the property several days a week. Waiting to see if they got mail was a significant source of excitement for the dozens of children who would spend the summer there.

The private park in the Horseshoe Bend area.

Forest Vacationers and Homesteaders

The Rim of the World Road was upgraded in the early 1920s, and the current route of Crest Forest Drive was chosen as the main route, so the amount of daily traffic was reduced through the Horseshoe Bend area. Horseshoe Bend was finally off the beaten path, and tranquility reigned.

By 1920, the yearly lease amount was up to twenty-five dollars, and eighteen new cabins were constructed. The tract was expanded, and the Great View area was added to the west of the Horseshoe Bend summer tract, expanding the number of lots from thirteen to forty-six on thirteen acres of land. "There is no place like it in the mountains," Bob Dubbell stated in a tract brochure.

Horseshoe Bend Repeatedly Attacked by Fires

Many fires have threatened the Horseshoe Bend ridge top area over the years. The Tuesday, July 25, 1911 fire that spared the Skyland area burned the chaparral away from the Horseshoe Bend summer tract just as many vacationers arrived for the season. By 10:00 p.m., the fire was directly below Horseshoe Bend. Volunteers from the valley were driven up the mountain to help the rangers who were overwhelmed by the one-hundred-degree temperatures and the winds. All the children and women along the crest were evacuated to the meadow in Little Bear Valley, while the men were called to duty, creating a firebreak amidst the brush, pine needles and pinecones.

By Sunday, the fire seemed under control. And then the winds started up again. According to newspaper reports at the time, some disgruntled Mexican volunteer firefighters set a couple small fires near Horseshoe Bend's Van Ness Springs, which spread just below the crest. The Skyland Resort Campgrounds were singed, some roofs of Pinecrest were on fire and had to be beat with wet blankets and the whole south face of the mountain was burning from Daley Canyon to Devil's Canyon. On Tuesday, the fire destroyed the new Incline Railroad, Strawberry Peak and the sawdust pile at the Baker Sawmill near Horseshoe Bend.

The September 23, 1919 fire started after the Horseshoe Bend vacationers had left for the season, as Labor Day was the end of their summer leases. The fire, which started in Miller Canyon near Pilot Rock, burned through Huston Flat timber, burned Knapp's Barn near Strawberry Peak and was only controlled by four hundred volunteers setting well-placed backfires. The volunteer firefighters were aided by well-timed fog and two inches of rain. Horseshoe Bend itself was spared. On June 12, 1920, over 125 newsmen drove up the Rim of the World Road on a three-day tour of the mountains.

They examined what was burned in the 1919 fire. Their first stops were Skyland and Horseshoe Bend, with their final mountain destination in Big Bear Valley.

Another fire affected the Horseshoe Bend area in the 1930s, burning some trees. The summer visitors always made their first activity of the season brush clearance to protect their beloved summer retreat from disaster.

The November 1980 Panorama Fire that began in Waterman Canyon seriously threatened the mountains. The final battleground to protect the mountain was at Horseshoe Bend. Fire engines were placed between the dwellings, with Dubbell's house used as command headquarters. Flames were shooting up hundreds of feet into the air and a 350-foot-tall pine became a giant torch when it caught on fire.

All looked bleak, and it appeared the fire would breach the rim and destroy the community of Crestline. Then the wind changed direction, and firefighters were able to keep the fire from establishing itself on the crest. Firemen at the scene said if the fire had broken through their line, the whole town of Crestline to the north might have been lost. Two homes were lost in Horseshoe Bend, but because of the covenants, conditions and restrictions (CC&Rs) of the new homeowners association, fire clearance had always been a requirement, and fire hydrants were installed when it joined the Crestline–Lake Arrowhead Water Agency in the 1970s.

The 2003 Old Fire severely affected the Horseshoe Bend community, where three homes were completely lost and others were partially burned. Again, firefighters stationed along the roadway between the houses fought the fire, turning back the flames and again protecting the entire community of Crestline.

Dubbell wrote in 1990:

> The original Horseshoe Bend property owners came from all walks of life; businessmen, professional people, doctors, ranchers, teachers and others. This was the blend of origins that created the solid base for the development and growth of Horseshoe Bend into the community it is today, a special place, one of a kind, well managed and protected from overzealous and indiscriminate development and erosion of values.

In 2009, a huge weekend-long party was held in Horseshoe Bends' private park, with most of the homeowners in attendance celebrating the 100th anniversary of the oldest summer tract in the San Bernardino Mountains.

IV

BEGINNING CRESTLINE

DART CANYON

Dart Canyon was named for one of the homesteading families who lived at the top of the canyon. Its name has often been misunderstood and called Dark Canyon; it has been listed with that name on several older-era maps. The Dark Canyon name may have referred to its dark north side canyon location, since all the trees make it very shadowy.

Dart Canyon is located northeast of Crestline, just past the Valley of the Moon. Dart Canyon Creek flows through the canyon to Silverwood Lake. Since the turn of the twentieth century, Dart Canyon has been an excellent apple-producing area with some ranches that have been producing apples for over one hundred years.

When S. Kenneth Josephs built a small dam across Dart Creek, forming a pond called Moon Lake, in Valley of the Moon in 1925, it created controversy, as water is a valuable resource for those in agriculture. The problem was soon negotiated and resolved. Because of its homesteaded beginnings, it was not incorporated into the Club San Moritz properties, which are next to it.

The apple orchards in the area were a well-known location to get apples for Halloween tricks during the 1950s. Former football player Andy Fletcher had a wonderful little apple- and flower-growing ranch in Dart Canyon. Many horse ranches still dot the tranquil, remote area, with weatherman Tom Hemphill of Community News and Weather running a stable at the north end of the road for many years.

Dart Canyon suffered from a flood after a heavy downpour in the 1990s that washed away a decades-old creek-side house.

Dart Canyon apple trees and an old wagon.

Frank Tetley Jr. inspects apple trees in the 1920s.

THE MISADVENTURES OF SAMUEL W. DILLIN, CRESTLINE'S FIRST POSTMASTER

It was 1917 when, sickly and weak, Samuel W. Dillin (pronounced De-Lynn) arrived in the San Bernardino Mountains from Chicago. The doctors at the Rush Medical College back east had determined that his persistent hacking cough was caused by a terminal disease. Samuel came west to die.

Dillin didn't have long to live when he arrived on a yellow auto stage to the broken-down front porch stage stop of the cement shed building at the crest of Arrowhead Reservoir Road that had formerly held sacks of cement for the building of the Little Bear Dam (now Lake Arrowhead Dam). He had only two dollars and fifty cents, a bedroll, a small tent, some food and his camera equipment. He did not even have enough money to cover his anticipated short life expectancy.

Dillin liked to talk and accidently met a man who was driving by. The man noticed Dillin's camera equipment and decided he wanted photos taken of his group, which was camping at Mormon Springs, nearby. It was Dillin's first day on the mountain and his first paying job. He earned twenty-one dollars that day, taking and printing the photos for the group of twenty-five campers. He decided the crest of the Rim of the World would be a good

The Arrowhead Reservoir Company's cement storage warehouse and stage stop, where Samuel Dillin arrived in 1917.

place to spend the remainder of what he figured were his few remaining days of life. It seemed like a wonderful place to die.

Dillin took a keg of the tasty water back with him from the Mormon Spring and later called it "an elixir of life." Within a year, Dillin claimed:

> *To realize that these big woods offer all the elements that make for health is a stimulant without price. It offers greater values than all the so-called tonics man ever invented. Its sweet ozone, sweet with fragrance of pine, in less than one year restored me to perfect health.*

Dillin turned the cement shed building, no longer needed by the Arrowhead Reservoir Company, into his base of operations for his photography business that first winter, living in the building and taking photographs of visitors to the crest area. When spring arrived, he decided he wasn't terminally ill after all, discovering that the altitude, fresh air and water agreed with him. He decided he loved it here and would happily spend the rest of his life in the mountains. He bought a lot next to a gurgling stream in Burnt Mill Canyon,

where he built a small cabin of cedar logs, with a big rock fireplace, finishing by late fall. He also set in a good supply of wood for the fireplace for the winter that was approaching. He lived there that winter, making friends with all the animals (squirrels and birds), while snowed in by over two feet of snow.

The local skunks also wanted to be his friend, but Dillin wasn't as welcoming to them, for obvious reasons. Late one clear but freezing night, the skunks entered the warmer-than-freezing cabin through a narrow crack between the logs, surprising and awakening Dillin. He very much wanted the whole family of skunks to leave, but he also didn't want to annoy them, "lest

Postmaster Samuel W. Dillin.

they leave a perfumed calling card." Dillin was known as a swift problem solver, so he quietly opened the door. Fortunately, when they saw the brilliant moonlight, they scampered outside to play. Dillin quickly closed and locked the door. The next day, he fixed that crack in the wall. He didn't want any more uninvited midnight visitors.

The next May, in 1919, Dillin, who now considered himself totally cured, accepted the job as postmaster of the Skyland Heights Post Office. It was located at the Skyland Resort and Campground office, which was also a Mountain Auto stage stop. The mail was delivered to the post office twice a week, and the locals would come get their mail on those days.

The Skyland Heights Post Office was not very busy during the winter. It was cold and lonely on the mountaintop during the winters in those days, as there were few year-round residents, and Skyland was difficult to reach when it snowed since it was located at the highest elevation of the area. He soon realized that the former cement shed down at the crest received a lot less snow because of its lower elevation.

One day, Dillin went down to San Bernardino for supplies, and on his way home from the stage stop (he walked most everywhere), he ran across a pair of huge mountain lion tracks in the snow. His twice-a-week walk from Skyland Heights Post Office to his home in Burnt Mill Canyon was eight miles long, but he was reveling in his good health, which he truly believed came from drinking the tasty, healthy waters from Mormon Springs and staying active.

A few days later, the snow was again falling on top of deep drifts, and Dillin was forced to meet the stage at the crest to get the mail (it then quickly returned to San Bernardino, not wanting to get stuck in the mountains). Dillin walked the mail up to the Skyland Heights Post Office and then waited for the locals to come get it.

Then he closed up the post office and left on foot for home (looking forward to sitting next to his warm fireplace) in Burnt Mill Canyon, some eight miles away. He took with him his warm coat and a flashlight, but not much else. He made this walk twice every week and didn't think much of it. He ate dinner at the Squirrel Inn and was at the rock arch at Pine Crest when it started to pour down rain. By the time he had reached the 101-Mile Marker on the rim, it was sleeting and snowing and very dark.

He carefully picked his way as he walked along the road, with which he was so familiar, suddenly discovering that a tree had fallen down across the route. He tried to walk around the length of the tree, since after turning on his flashlight and looking at the huge tree he quickly decided it would be too difficult to climb over it. So he walked around to the closest end and then suddenly fell into the cavity at the base where the roots had been.

Upon self-inspection, he instantly surmised three things. First, although shaken up, he was not really injured. Second, the hole was large and seemed to shelter him from the storm, but he still intended to get himself out and go home.

And third, unfortunately for Dillin, the two mountain lions whose paw prints he had seen just days before were using that same cavity in the ground as their shelter from the storm, and they did not seem to be in a mood to share with him, protesting loudly his arrival. He was instantly frightened at this predicament. He quickly realized he was stuck in this hole with two mountain lions, which didn't want to share their shelter from the storm. In the darkness, he couldn't see an easy escape route for himself. He knew no one would be passing this way in the storm:

> *Why they failed to attack me, I do not know, unless their extreme struggle through the sleet and snow had reduced their fighting strength to a low ebb. Why, oh why, will an experienced mountaineer commit such a blunder to leave civilization for the wilderness without a match?*

Dillin whined to himself and then remembered he had a flashlight. He turned it on, and the hissing cats began to strike out with their paws. Maybe that wasn't such a good idea was his first reaction. Then the cats suddenly shrank back against the opposite wall of the cave, still loudly threatening him.

He tried to distract the wildcats and desperately looked to escape from the cave. He knew staying in the hole was not an option. He saw some roots that might be climbed, if he could get to them. He inched his way toward the roots, which he hoped he could climb and make his exit, but he slipped in the mud and fell.

This startled the cats, which screamed and rushed toward him.

They leapt over him toward the back of the cave. As he scrambled to get up out of the mud, he kept the light shining in their eyes. He made his way to the roots and quickly climbed out of the hole and ran up the road, fearful they were nipping at his heels. Fortunately, the frightened mountain lions did not follow him as he ran through the storm. In his haste, Dillin became lost in the blowing snowstorm somewhere around Daley Canyon Road.

Dillin wandered, trying to find his way home, not able to see more than a few feet in front of himself, until near midnight when he finally saw a stone chimney through the fog and storm. Then all his energy left him as his adrenaline rush stopped. Dillin had to practically crawl to the house, which was fortunately unlocked. He entered the unoccupied house totally exhausted from the hours of storm, exposure and mountain lion encounter.

He hoped he would survive, but he felt as though he were losing the fight against the elements. He didn't even make a mental list of all the mistakes he had made that evening, for he felt that might verify that he didn't deserve to have found this deserted cabin. He didn't yet consider that he was trespassing and that he could be arrested; he was just relieved he was inside, out of the storm.

This was before electricity came to the mountain, and it was dark and freezing cold inside the cabin. Dillin could not light a fire in the fireplace because he still didn't have a match, and he wasn't sure his frozen fingers would have been able to hold one anyway. He found some blankets, removed his drenched clothes and wrapped his wet, shivering body in them. It took at least an hour to defrost enough to get to sleep.

The morning arrived bright and sunny, but he found his clothes were frozen solid. He began to look around the summer vacation cabin and was able to start a fire after finally finding matches. They were sitting next to a bottle of Scotch whiskey, from which he later swore he took only one drink, "for his health." He didn't want to take advantage of the owner of this safe haven he had found, although he thought he surely needed and deserved more, after what he had been through the previous night. He felt fortunate the cabin's owners were not there because how would he, a respected postmaster, explain his naked condition in a stranger's cabin?

With the fire going, he went back to sleep with the blanket warmly wrapped around him as his clothes dried next to the fire until 3:00 p.m. He then got up and cleaned up the small mess he had made, even folding the blankets. He left, securing the cabin, which he had found unlocked. He didn't want anyone to break in and steal anything from this place that had saved his life. He went home to his own cabin, which was only a half mile away. He stayed next to his warm fireplace for two days, recovering from his terrifying mountain lion ordeal.

As he returned to the post office, he saw that the hole at the base of the fallen log had caved in, and he wondered whether the mountain lions had escaped or perished. He hoped for their safety, although he also hoped to never meet up with them again.

Samuel W. Dillin opened a store at the cement shed building at the corner of what are now Highway 138 and Crest Forest Drive and moved the Skyland Heights Post Office down to it in the spring of 1919. He rebuilt the shed into a big room for a grocery store and his photography business, with

This former Arrowhead Reservoir Company's cement shed building became Dillin's store in 1919.

an amusement hall in back, and the post office was placed in a room added to the west side of the building.

Postmaster Dillin applied for a name change, since he had moved the post office from Skyland Heights. He chose the name "Crestline" from Guernsey's now-defunct development since it was in common usage for the area. He painted the new name in big red letters over the door. That is how Crestline officially got its name.

Dillin built an amusement hall behind the grocery store that became the Tavern, where visitors could "pass an evening in leisure." It was known for its thirty-six-foot-long dance floor. The Tavern had a rustic, long front porch with repaired steps that were no longer broken like when he had arrived two years earlier. The stage still stopped twice a week, so it was the first building most visitors saw when arriving at the crest, and they would stop and enter.

Dillin promoted the health of the clean lifestyle and the excellent water of the mountain, which he attributed to his longevity. He wrote in one of his many pamphlets:

> *If you are ill or broken in health from overwork, a few weeks in this nearby community will not only restore you, but add years to your life, for have not I, who lived so near to shadowland, drawn both inspiration and health from its rugged solitude?*

Dillin was postmaster of the Crestline Post Office until 1929, developing the store and tavern, and he watched the town and village of Crestline grow

Mormon Springs plaque. Dillin claimed that the water from the spring cured him.

up around him. He published many pamphlets about his adventures and promoting Crestline. Developers Mann and Ramsey began to subdivide the property into cabin sites around the post office and encouraged the businesses in Crestline Village to grow. Charles S. Mann became Crestline's postmaster in 1929, and he continued in that position until 1935.

By then, the area of Crestline was no longer the wild forest to which sickly Samuel W. Dillin had arrived on a stage to die in 1917 but rather a growing community with businesses (some with electricity), a chamber of commerce, the Crest Forest School and many year-round residents and hundreds of seasonal vacationers driving up a paved High Gear Road that allowed privately owned automobiles to easily access the heights.

CHRONOLOGY OF CRESTLINE POST OFFICES

In our mountains, prior to a post office being established, friends delivered letters when they traveled up or down the mountain. Post offices were requested after people had settled permanently in an area.

When a post office was officially established for the purpose of serving the residents and tourists of the area, the Postmaster General's Office often changed the commonly used name or spelling of the name of the area. One reason might be that another town in the state was using the same or a similar name. It was often the case in these mountains that the postmaster general thought the creative subdivision names submitted were too long or cumbersome for a postmark. This occurred frequently as local mountain post offices were established.

Incline: 1907

In the West End Mountain District, called Pineland at the time, John Hansen established the first post office at the Skyland Heights Resort in June 1907. The Skyland Heights area began as a camping area in the 1890s and became a campground and resort in 1906 with the construction of the Skyland Lodge, coinciding with the opening of the former Arrowhead Reservoir Company Toll Road to free public usage.

The post office was named "Incline" because it was near the upper terminus of the newly built Incline Railroad cable car system built by the Arrowhead Reservoir Company to transport its bags of cement up the face of the mountain (since it no longer had exclusive use of the former toll road) for building a dam in Little Bear Valley (to create Lake Arrowhead). It was anticipated that the unique incline rail system would become a tourist method of arrival at the Skyland Resort (like it had on Mount Lowe above Pasadena), which is the reason for the post office's name. It was hoped that the postmark name itself might encourage visitors to the area to mail postcards. Walter Hubbard became postmaster in June 1909. When the Incline Railway fell into disuse because it didn't work well, the name of the post office was changed to Skyland Heights in 1910.

Skyland Heights: 1910

The post office was still just a room located in the general store at Skyland Heights Resort and Campground and retained James Hattery, who had become postmaster in November 1909 at the Incline Post Office, but he only lasted the winter and left in April 1910, when Louise Newton became postmaster. Because the resort was popular and the Incline was out of use, the name change was appropriate. Having a location from which to mail postcards was popular and promoted business at the resort. Many of the postcards were original photographs of the people sending them, created by a professional photographer who lived in the area during the summer season. One popular scene that was photographed would be a group of family or friends who would have their picture taken in one of the "picture-frame trees" and have it made into a postcard, a sort of a "don't you wish you were here" statement.

In 1910, the Skyland Heights Post Office was the only post office west of Fredalba (near Running Springs). The post office also provided mail service to the sawmills in the area; the homesteaders in Seely Flats and Dart Canyon, who were growing apples and other items; and other resorts such as Pinecrest, Squirrel Inn, Thousand Pines and the Arrowhead Reservoir Company.

The Skyland Heights Inn, Resort and General Store conveniently had picture postcards of the area to sell and mail, which cost a penny to send in 1910. The resort not only offered camping but also had cabins for rent, and the inn's lodging, including food, cost $2.50 a day.

The post office continued with a new postmaster assigned almost yearly. William Dougherty came in May 1913, followed by Ara Roxborough in

The Incline and Skyland Heights Post Office building at the Skyland Inn.

November of that year. Next came Mattie Woodall in October 1916 and Allie Keller in March 1918 until 1919, when Samuel W. Dillin became postmaster in May. It was cold and lonely in the mountains during the winters in those days, as there were few year-round residents who needed mail service. Skyland Heights was at the highest elevation of the area, making it difficult to reach in poor weather.

Crestline: 1919

Samuel W. Dillin opened a photography/general store/tavern at the corner of what are now Highway 138 and Crest Forest Drive. Dillin got the approval of the eighteen postal subscribers of the Skyland Heights area and moved the post office down to that building, which was already designated as a stage stop in 1919.

Postmaster Dillin applied to change the name of the Skyland Heights Post Office, stating there was postal confusion with other post offices with similar names—Skyland Wright in Northern California and another Skyland in Central California—so mail was constantly delayed when delivered to the wrong area. Besides, the new location was no longer at the Skyland Inn.

Crestline's first post office is on right side of Dillin's building.

Beginning Crestline

Dillin chose the name of Crestline, which was in usage for the crest area. The post office was located in a small building he built, attached to his general store and the Crestline Tavern. Crestline's developer, Charles S. Mann, was postmaster after Dillin, from 1929 to 1935.

Moonlake: 1929

In October 1929 (before the stock market crash in December), Frederick (Fritz) Muller, a retired foundry worker, opened a post office in the Arthur Gregory subdevelopment of Valley of the Moon. Muller wanted to call the post office "Arrowhead Valley," after the Arrowhead Valley Club, which was well established in the Valley of the Moon area, but the postmaster general rejected the name, as there were already several Arrowhead post offices in the area. Lake Arrowhead Post office opened in 1924, and Arrowhead Springs began using the name in 1887. There was also the Arrowhead Post Office in north San Bernardino, and the Arrow Bear Post Office opened in 1927. So potential confusion with an Arrowhead Valley Post office was a real possibility.

The two-word name "Moon Lake" was Muller's second choice (named after the local lake), but the words were smashed together into the one-word "Moonlake" name for the post office. The office was located in Muller's building near the Arrowhead Valley Lodge's clubhouse.

It is said that Muller would trudge through the snow during the winter to get the mail across the Huston Flat to his post office (three miles away from the Crestline office at the top of the mountain) when the roads were closed. Muller enjoyed being postmaster and did it as a full-time hobby, for "something to do," although he did accept the tiny fourth-class postmaster's salary. He maintained the post office, even after the demise of the Arrowhead Valley Club and the many foreclosures in the Valley of the Moon area during the Depression, for the homesteaders who were growing apples in Dart Canyon.

Switzerland: 1939

After Lake Gregory was completed and filled with water in 1938, Frederick Muller applied to change the name of the Moonlake Post Office to reflect the new Swiss image of the area. The Club San Moritz had remodeled the former Arrowhead Valley Clubhouse, and the Lake Gregory Lake and Land Company was beginning to develop the area around the new lake.

The San Bernardino Mountain communities were beginning to promote themselves as the "Alps of Southern California," so Muller chose the name of Switzerland, which was approved in May 1939. The Switzerland name was short-lived because when Muller died in 1941, the post office was closed. Postal service for the San Moritz and Valley of the Moon areas was transferred to the Crestline Post Office.

The 1929 dirt roads had improved and were paved by 1941, and private cars were prevalent, so residents were able to get to the Crestline Post Office.

CRESTLINE POST OFFICE MOVES AND ENLARGES AS CRESTLINE GROWS

The Crestline Post Office, which had remained in the Crestline Tavern while Charles S. Mann was postmaster, was moved to the Summerhouse Saloon building in the mid-1930s when Frederick Smith became postmaster in October 1935, still in the uptown area (Lake Gregory was not yet completed). The mail service from the Valley of the Moon's Switzerland Post Office was added to Crestline's service area in 1941, after Frederick Muller's death, increasing the size of the Crestline Post Office to almost one hundred boxes. During the war years of 1943–46, Cedarpines Park's mail was also temporarily delivered to the Crestline office, since the Cedarpines Park Post Office was temporarily closed when its postmaster left for the war.

In 1948, while Mary Tipton Fry was postmaster, the post office facility was moved east three blocks along Crest Forest Drive to the "government building" near Fern Drive. It now had over one hundred locking post office boxes and a long list of general delivery names. Sometimes, especially during the summer months, the wait in line for general delivery mail could take up to an hour.

The Crestline Post Office remained in the uptown area until 1963, when a modern building on Knapp's Cutoff at the corner of Lake Drive and Old Mill Road was built especially for the library to use, housing 1,500 boxes. It was predicted that this building would be able to handle any growth that would occur in Crestline for the foreseeable future.

Unfortunately, this would prove not to be true.

V

CRESTLINE RESORTS AND DEVELOPMENTS

VALLEY OF ENCHANTMENT

The Valley of Enchantment, located north and west of Crestline, has been a popular area, used throughout the ages by many different people. The Serrano Indians originally found the meadow and weather to their liking for a summer retreat from the heat of the desert. There is evidence that they returned for over five thousand years, collecting acorns, nuts and berries and living under the trees in the meadow along Seeley Creek.

Then, David Seely and other loggers found easy access to the area and a good variety of trees to their liking, with a steady stream of water to power their sawmills. The valley area was cut over by several different lumbering operations—including the William LaPraix, Joseph Tyler, Jacobs and Excelsior Sawmills—over a period of almost fifty years.

Assemblyman Byron Waters, a rich San Bernardino lawyer, homesteaded the area as a retreat from the city below, planting apple trees, some of which are still producing today. Waters, who lived on Seely Flat for over twenty-five years, was getting older and wished to divide some of his land and sell it since he was going blind. The City of Los Angeles chose the valley to build a year-round campground for its citizens to visit and escape the big city. Camp Seeley is still operating today.

Then, in the 1920s, California highway commissioner Frank A. Tetley Sr. bought most of Waters's property adjoining Camp Seeley to build a subdivision for vacationers to enjoy the mountains. Because Tetley was savvy about promotion, and since the Rim of the World Road was well known,

Frank A. Tetley Sr. developed Rim of the World Park/Valley of Enchantment.

he called his development Rim of the World Park, although the area was actually several miles away from the Rim of the World Road.

He developed the area by cutting in roads, securing water rights (a specialty of his), drilling wells and bringing electricity to the area as soon as it was available. He connected to the phone line that John Adams had strung to the area in 1919. He divided the property into twenty-five- by fifty-foot lots. These lots today are considered "substandard" by the county but at the time were large enough to pitch a tent or build a small vacation cabin. These lots were originally sold for only twenty-five dollars each, with an easy payment plan. They sold quickly, with every lot having water service, and eventually three annexes were added to the original subdivision. Because of Tetley's position on the board of directors of Citizens Bank in Riverside, it was possible for him to get loans for improvements and upgrades and to maintain solvency during the tough years of the early 1930s.

A small village was constructed with businesses such as a grocery store, restaurants, a real estate office, stables, a gas station and others, which helped anchor the homes.

Tetley believed from past experience that water was the most important element for the success of the venture. He laid out the water lines, paid for the mules and laborers to dig the ditches and dug horizontal wells into the mountainside. He owned the water company but turned it into a mutual water company as soon as there were enough shareholders to make the water company viable. Valley of Enchantment Mutual Water Company, incorporated in 1927, is still in existence today. By 1932, Tetley had sold 1,167 shares of the 1,500 available water shares. (Several other mountain subdivisions went broke during this same period).

Compliments of F. A. TETLEY
Owner of
Rïm of the World Park

These apples are picked from the apple orchard at the RIM OF THE WORLD PARK. The trees have never been irrigated or pruned, and they are waiting patiently for someone to purchase the lots upon which they are grown, who will give them the proper attention and build a home upon the lots.

They are always two enjoyable times among the apple trees, when they are in bloom in the spring on account of the fragance and beauty, and in the fall when the apples are ripe.

The small sack of apples is presented to the home and lot owners in the tract, and while they are not large, I hope you will enjoy them. They are good either raw, cooked, or made into cider.

Lots of Good Wishes and we hope to see you often this fall and winter.

This bag for apples advertised Rim of the World Park.

The name of the development was changed from Rim of the World Park to Valley of Enchantment during the early 1930s because of the confusion between Tetley's development and Rim of the World Tract, located in Crest Park. Besides, it was not on the rim or close to the highway, and it was located in a valley, so the new advertising brochures said in small print, "Rim of the World Park located in the Beautiful VALLEY OF ENCHANTMENT." The last part was in large print, introducing the new name.

Because of his frequent trips to the mountains, when Governor Rolf appointed Tetley as a state road commissioner, the improvement of the Rim of the World Highway into a "high-gear" paved road was at the top of his list. It was relocated along the southern face of the mountain to maximize natural snowmelt to reduce the amount of plowing needed. He even received the honor of cutting the ribbon during the Rim of the World High Gear Highway dedication ceremony on October 21, 1933. This improvement eliminated the switchback section of the road from Panorama Point to Crest

Ohrmund's Resort and campground was in the Valley of Enchantment.

Forest Drive. It then became known as the High Gear Road and was highly praised. If it hadn't been for the Depression, the mountain resorts would have immediately grown with these improved and paved access roads.

During the 1940s, Ohrmund's Campground and Resort opened for camping and the exclusive Club San Moritz opened its Pitch and Putt Golf center in the Valley of Enchantment.

VALLEY OF THE MOON

Valley of the Moon and Moon Lake

The Valley of the Moon is a hidden wonder located just off the beaten path in a little valley just over the rise from Huston Flat and at the top of Dart (aka Miller) Canyon.

The first time Valley of the Moon was thought about—other than by the Indians, who knew it was a wonderful camping location under the oak trees and next to the stream, or the early lumbermen, who cut trees for their sawmills—was in the 1890s when the Arrowhead Reservoir Company saw the small valley downhill from its water project as a perfect location for

70

another reservoir as a part of its seven-lake project to bring water to the San Bernardino Valley for agricultural purposes.

The Arrowhead Reservoir Project purchased logging tracts with a plan to flood them, creating water storage lakes as the water flowed downhill to the San Bernardino Valley. Although a tunnel was drilled toward the Valley of the Moon (not yet named) with the intention of flooding it, the tunnel was never finished, so the beautiful treed area was not made into a lake bottom.

With the closure of the Arrowhead Reservoir Project because of the death of James Mooney in 1919, the land tracts were then offered for sale. Redlands citrus grower Arthur Gregory bought some of the property to build sawmills to cut the trees for wooden boxes so he could send his fruit to market. He also soon jumped on the bandwagon with other land developers and offered some of it as vacation property.

The Dart Canyon area was already growing apples on some of the homesteaded lands from the early 1900s downstream from the future Valley of the Moon.

In 1924, Arthur Gregory and A.G. Hamilton (of Fontana) and their wives subdivided the already logged and burned-over logging tract, just east of Huston Flat off the road to Dart Canyon. They sold the land, which they described as beginning to "scrub with oaks and cedars," and choice lots in the area that they decided to call Valley of the Moon.

S. Kenneth Josephs built a small dam across Dart Creek near the head of Miller Canyon, forming a pond called Moon Lake in 1925. Moon Lake was really not more than a shallow pond, a little over an acre in size. Despite the size, it still caused a lot of concern for the apple ranchers who lived downstream in Dart Canyon, as they feared the loss of the water for their orchards. The controversy was soon negotiated and put aside, and many of the orchards remain to this day. Most estimates put Moon Lake not deeper than six feet. It was deep enough for canoes and fishing during the summer and shallow enough to freeze over for ice-skating in the winter some years. It was a scenic and recreational economic asset to the area for tourism, and a motel was built across the street that was frequently used by members of the Arrowhead Valley Club and their friends.

The fourth-class Moonlake Post Office was opened by Fritz Muller in a small house in the Valley of the Moon in 1929, described as one-eighth of a mile west of Dart Creek. Muller was very dedicated to his postal customers, many of them year-round residents and longtime homesteaders living in Dart Canyon.

Fritz Muller was postmaster of the Moonlake Post Office from October 1929 until October 1939, when he requested a name change to Switzerland to compliment the newly opened Club San Moritz located in the Valley of the Moon. He continued to operate the Switzerland Post Office until his death in 1941.

Arrowhead Valley Club

As the lots sold, in 1926, S. Kenneth Josephs built a private lodge and resort named the Arrowhead Valley Club. The name Arrowhead Valley Club reflected the hidden aspect of the club's location, as visitors had to take the road toward Arrowhead Village and then turn off and come down into a "hidden valley" from Strawberry (Twin Peaks).

In 1926, a special part of the Valley of the Moon subdivision was laid out exclusively for Masons to purchase so they could vacation together in an alpine setting. It was less than a year later that a Masonic Installation of Officers was held in the Arrowhead Valley Club's lodge building.

The Arrowhead Valley Club was a private, restricted social club, as was typical for the era. But members often invited their friends to come with them and join in the activities. Friends could stay at the motel across the street.

In 1929, the yearly registration fee for the club, after membership approval by the board of advisors, was $24.50. A life membership was $200.00. The board

Arrowhead Valley Club and Moon Lake.

Crestline Resorts and Developments

The massive local stone fireplace inside the main room of the Arrowhead Valley Club.

of advisors was made up of distinguished gentlemen of the time, including W.A. Shay, sheriff of San Bernardino County and an undersheriff and judge from Los Angeles County; movie stars Harry Langdon and Arthur Clayton; and director Arthur Ripley. The board included insurance and mortgage agents, doctors, attorneys and the future governor of California San Francisco mayor James Rolph Jr.; local forest ranger Bert Switzer; and San Bernardino judge D.E. Van Leuven. It can be assumed that with such respectable men involved in the venture, it was a solid investment and a club worth joining.

The club had a beautiful rustic log interior, boasting the largest stone fireplace in the state, made from over 160 tons of rocks and other materials. The main room was decorated with deer heads, snowshoes and other "mountain-y elements" and had furnishings handcrafted from logs. Inside, it featured a billiard room, a dance floor and piano and dining facilities.

Some outside activities included horseback riding with riding instructor Ray Walters, archery on the archery range and hiking in the clear, cool air available at the "healthy altitude" under the forest trees. The club promoted its Moon Lake shore location and the fine fishing, canoeing and (in the winter) ice-skating.

It had a rustic pine plank exterior with log accents. The exterior deck that almost went around the building, with beautiful vistas from any location, had log railings that could support canvas awnings if the sun ever got too hot.

The Arrowhead Valley Club had extensive building plans to erect a new clubhouse that was to supersede the current one. The designs drawn up showed the lodge building would be at least four times larger and less rustic, more in the "mission style" of a grand resort of the era.

The 1929 map showed how easy access to the area was since the High Gear Road was nearing completion. The directions to Arrowhead Valley included taking the High Gear Road past Arrowhead Highlands and going past the Squirrel Inn, toward Lake Arrowhead, then turning left at Strawberry Flats (near current-day Twin Peaks) and traveling down present-day Arosa Road (which was an old lumbering road) to the Valley of the Moon. Following those directions, going up almost all the way up to Strawberry Peak and then down, Valley of the Moon must have really felt like a secret valley!

Since many families still did not own private automobiles in the 1920s, Mountain Transit Lines was used to get to the resort. The Arrowhead Valley Club had a few rooms for the members to stay in, with the luxury of sinks in the rooms, but most stayed at the hotel across the street.

One couple, Ed and Marjorie, regularly visited the Arrowhead Valley Club as guests of an Arrowhead Valley Club member. They would make their reservations at the motel across from the lodge for two nights, spending Saturday, leisurely, at Moon Lake, doing some of the many activities available and then joining their friends for dinner and the dance at the club that evening. They met so many nice people and enjoyed the mountain life so much that, years later, they bought property and moved to the mountains. They are an example of just one of thousands of families who have moved to the mountains as a result of vacationing in the area.

"Chief" Jones (center) was the Arrowhead Valley Club's archery instructor in the mid-1920s.

Crestline Resorts and Developments

The Arrowhead Valley Club, with its fine plans, distinguished board of advisors and excellent facilities disappointingly did not have a long life (less than ten years) because when the New York Stock Market fell in 1929 and the Depression hit, all the mountain resorts suffered greatly. Many people had bought their property on the monthly payment plan, and when their jobs went and they could not afford the payments, the developer or the bank would foreclose on the property. Also, the state could take the land for any unpaid property taxes. Valley of the Moon had many properties foreclosed on. The Arrowhead Valley Club closed its doors. The Threatt family ran the large lodge building for a few years during the Depression as a boardinghouse, and that usage protected the building from squatters.

The Valley of the Moon area did not die completely, however. In fact, in 1933, the Crestline Chamber of Commerce sponsored an end-of-summer bash called "Paradise Gulch." It was held in the Valley of the Moon, outside the lodge building, just months after the end of Prohibition and sponsored by a beer company. Afterward, the sheriff said, "If ANY other parties of THAT kind are to be held again, I'll have to close them in advance!" It was obvious that the crowd was a bit too drunk and rowdy for the sheriff. (See chapter on Paradise Gulch.)

It was not until 1938 that a new investment group purchased the lodge building and properties, creating a new private, exclusive resort club in the old Arrowhead Valley Club building. They remodeled the building to create a Swiss alpine feel and convinced Muller to apply for a new name for the post office, changing it to Switzerland to reflect their new image. He was for any development that would help the area escape from the Depression attitude, which had affected the area for so long. They called the area the "Alps of Southern California." The new resort was called the Club San Moritz.

The Alps of Southern California

The "Alps of Southern California" was an advertising slogan used to describe the San Bernardino Mountains beginning in the later part of the 1930s. The Club San Moritz brought the Swiss Alps concept to the San Bernardino Mountains as the effects of the Great Depression were beginning to wane. Club San Moritz began in 1938 in the building that had formerly housed the Arrowhead Valley Club, which was remodeled into European chateau style.

The club named its subdivision Switzerland, and the post office name was soon switched from Moon Lake to Switzerland. The new streets built in the enlarged subdivision all had names from the Alps, such as Chateau and Berne, and continued as the subdivision grew; a new lodge building was built next to Lake Gregory in the early 1950s. Street names like Jungfrau, Zurich and Zuger were also added, as the Switzerland Subdivision moved west of the lakeshore and began butting against the Crestline Subdivision of Charles S. Mann. Now it is difficult to see the original dividing lines between the two subdivisions, as they have merged, becoming the Lake Gregory Village area.

ARROWHEAD HIGHLANDS

Arrowhead Highlands on the High Gear Road

During the 2003 Old Fire, as the firefighters were stretched along Highway 18 protecting the mountain communities, the decision was made to save the closed Cliffhanger Restaurant at Arrowhead Highlands, as it was a landmark and had historical value. Why would they want to save an empty building?

Located on the south side of State Highway 18, near the signaled intersection of Lake Gregory Drive and Highway 189, the Cliffhanger is the first building a person encounters when driving up Highway 18 after passing Waterman Canyon, some ten miles away. Arrowhead Highlands forms a gateway to both the Crest Forest and Lake Arrowhead areas.

The Cliffhanger building sits perched on the edge of a rocky precipice of the rim, overlooking the valley below. On a clear day, you can see all the way to Catalina, an island twenty-six miles off the coast of California. It has a prime location that epitomizes the image that the "Rim of the World Highway" promises in its name. It sits next to a tall rock outcropping, Sphinx Rock, whose profile looks somewhat like the Egyptian sphinx. Sphinx Rock was where Crest Drive came out to kiss the rim, and its beautiful views curved away from the edge toward Squirrel Inn and Little Bear Valley (Lake Arrowhead).

The silent movie companies used Sphinx Rock in their productions, noticing this scenic location not far from the resorts of the Squirrel Inn and Pinecrest. In the 1916 movie *The Eyes of the World*, the actors chased each other around Sphinx Rock and fought on top of it. The movie company employed nets below the rocks and used stunt men, but one stunt man almost missed the nets when he fell.

Crestline Resorts and Developments

Sphinx Rock and Cliffhanger Restaurant were used as sets in the movie *Next* (2007), starring Nicholas Cage.

The U.S. Forest Service rangers had used the rock outcropping as an initiation location, where new rangers had to quickstep on top of the "head" part of the rock (but without nets). It became so popular that, in 1914, the rangers began doing it for fun so the tourists could photograph them.

Lee's Arrowhead Highlands Café

When the 1920s arrived and saw the subdivision of the forested lands of the mountain into vacation, camping and homesites, this area was a logical location to develop because of its scenic beauty. Arrowhead Highlands subdivision was envisioned as a resort location, with a clubhouse, pool and view lots, and was a stopping point as Crest Drive reached the rim at the juncture of the new High Gear Road in 1929. The name Arrowhead Highlands came from its location, high above the valley, some five thousand feet below and "near" the new Lake Arrowhead Village development, which had opened in 1924.

Lee's Café was constructed, in the mid-1920s, in the original half of the current Cliffhanger Restaurant building. The store advertised: "Eats, drinks, smokes and rest rooms." It had a gas pump out front and a lunch counter inside. That A-frame building is the center of the current Cliffhanger's structure.

The gas pump was expanded into a garage, as early automobiles would often need mechanical help by the time they reached the crest. Lee's Café and Garage was the first building on the High Gear Road (Highway 18) after the road passed through what is now called "The Narrows." When the High Gear Road was initially approved, it was assumed that the Arrowhead

Lee's Café and the Arrowhead Highlands store in the late 1920s.

Highlands connection to Crest Forest Drive would be the new entrance to Crestline (this was before the Crest Forest Chamber of Commerce convinced the San Bernardino Board of Supervisors to build the road, now known as Highway 138, in 1929).

Lee's Café was a popular stopping place when arriving in the mountains and was very distinctive with the area's name painted on the roof. Travelers couldn't miss it by the High Gear Road.

Arrowhead Highlands: "A Kingdom of Pines"

The 1920s saw the subdividing of the privately held forested lands of the mountain into vacation, camping and homesites. Arrowhead Highlands was a desirable place to develop due to its beautiful views all the way to the ocean almost one hundred miles away.

The Arrowhead Highlands Subdivision began in the late 1920s around the Arrowhead Highlands Club, which was located on the knoll between the Rim of the World Drive (now known as Crest Forest Drive) and the newly cut High Gear Road (now known as "The Narrows"), at the elevation of 5,400 feet. Arrowhead Highlands' promotional brochure boasted:

> *Shrewd buyers chose Arrowhead Highlands, not only for its natural beauty and unsurpassed views of the purple deserts to the north combined with the great expanse of the fertile valley to the south with its sixteen cities.*

Crestline Resorts and Developments

The Clubhouse was rustic in appearance, a very popular style for that era, equipped for the convenience of the club members. It was advertised with "a kitchen, and dining room facilities where home-cooked food may be enjoyed by members at a minimum of expense," and was stocked with canned food items for members to purchase for their lodge- or cabin-cooked meals. The restaurant featured meals at seventy-five cents for lunch or dinner. The Clubhouse had "a spacious fireplace, which lends an air of comfort to the club-room surroundings."

The Arrowhead Highlands Company was located on Western Avenue in Los Angeles. With the purchase of a lot in the subdivision, a free life membership in the Arrowhead Highlands Club was given (a common practice of the time). The club promised to never assess any dues for the use of the club facilities by property owners. Promotional materials said a new, larger clubhouse would be built as the subdivision grew and demand for additional facilities increased.

The Arrowhead Highlands Club had "mountain lodges" (cabins) with cooking facilities for rent for its members. At the rate of $3.00 a day for two persons, a lodge that slept six cost $7.50 a day, with special weekly and monthly rates available. There were also a couple hotel rooms inside the clubhouse for rent. These facilities and amenities reflected those offered at other resorts and private clubs (such as the Arrowhead Valley Club over in Valley of the Moon) at the time.

The promotional brochures of this era are fun to read. The ads for Arrowhead Highlands were especially flowery in their language and hype:

> *Arrowhead Highlands is a kingdom of stately pines in the center of the greatest recreational development on the Pacific Coast. Millions of dollars have been spent in the San Bernardino Mountains on rustic homes, clubs, hotels, business establishments and community improvements. Splendid mountain roads wind in and out through picturesque communities created by man for his pleasure, health and profit.*

The brochure continued:

> *Arrowhead Highlands, situated at an elevation of 5,400 feet...is a vast district above the smoke and bustle of the great sea level cities. This kingdom among the pines is an irresistible lure that draws hundreds of thousands to its domain of happiness every year.*
>
> *Arrowhead Highlands is the only resort from which it is possible to command unsurpassed views of the purple desert to the north, combined*

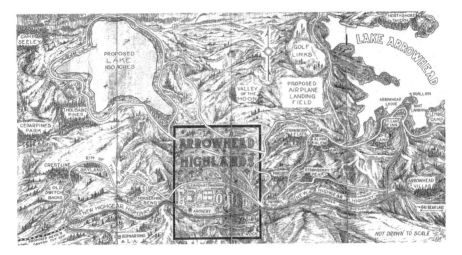

This map of Arrowhead Highlands shows the proposed Lake Gregory in the 1930s.

with the great expanse of the fertile valley on the south, with the sixteen cities that are seen from the Arrowhead Highlands Clubhouse. Nowhere will you find a spot so favored by Nature, so ideally fashioned by her for the enjoyment of mankind, as is Arrowhead Highlands.

The eloquently written brochure convinced many of the benefits of mountain resort living. It was honest in one superlative statement, to be sure: "Arrowhead Highlands Was Perfectly Located with Fabulous Views!"

The subdivision's recreation facilities included the Clubhouse, a swimming pool, tennis courts, a stable, horseshoe-pitching courts and an archery range. Its brochure also promoted all the recreational opportunities the mountain could offer, such as boating, fishing, croquet, bridge, dancing, ice-skating, skiing and tobogganing, somewhat indicating that they were available at the resort. However, these activities were actually offered at the nearby Lake Arrowhead Village resort. Apparently, in their zeal to impress buyers, those 1920s real estate promoters tended to exaggerate a bit.

The Cliffhanger Building

The fact that the landmark Cliffhanger building still exists today is a tribute to the brave firefighters who decided to fight the flames of an out-of-control wildfire and protect the building—twice—during the last thirty years, once during the 1980 Panorama Fire and again during the 2003 Old Fire.

Crestline Resorts and Developments

The original building was built next to Sphinx Rock in the 1920s, as a convenience store for travelers, with "eats, drinks, smokes and rest rooms," which were the words emblazoned on the wall of the building. It had a large parking lot, and on the roof was painted, "Arrowhead Highlands," in huge, bold lettering. Quite distinctive and memorable, in a gaudy way, it really stood out in contrast to the natural trees. It was perfectly situated on the rim and just at the "right time and distance" for a break from driving.

Lee's Café became many families' traditional stopping and luncheon location along the High Gear Road, on the way to the Lake Arrowhead area. Lee's Café, as it was known, was a good place to stop, enjoy the fabulous view and stretch one's legs. Lee's Café served hot meals at the lunch counter for seventy-five cents, and the scenic location, gift shop and restrooms encouraged many motorists to stop "to cool their engines" after the long drive up the steep mountain. Soon, because of the long drive and the mechanical nature of automobiles, the gas pump was expanded into an automotive repair garage with a "mechanic on duty." Later on, a garage building was constructed next door to the Arrowhead Highlands store, with the name "Lee's Garage" painted on the roof. On clear days, which were frequent in the 1920s through the '40s, a person could see all the way to Catalina Island, twenty-six miles off the coast, out in the Pacific Ocean. What a publicity lure!

As the years progressed, the café and gift store building was added on to, and the attic area was upgraded with dormers. Another room was added to the café when the lunchroom was expanded. Traffic increased as more people bought private autos and the economy boomed.

Soon, the Arrowhead Highlands subdivision added a tract office building next to Lee's Garage and Café, emphasizing its view of Catalina Island. "Location, Location, Location"—the property practically sold itself. People wanted vacation property in the mountains to escape the heat of the valley during those long hot summers before air conditioning was invented, until the Depression arrived.

The amount of traffic passing Arrowhead Highlands slowed during the Depression years of the 1930s. But travel through the area never totally stopped, as movie companies, Hollywood stars and other affluent persons continued to visit Lake Arrowhead's resorts, and they often stopped at Lee's for gas and food or just to look at the view.

The 1930s saw the demise of the Arrowhead Highlands Resort and subdivision due to underfunding and taxes. The highly touted expansion, upgrades and paving of the subdivision's roads never occurred, and one

Lee's Coffee Shop at Arrowhead Highlands in the 1950s.

of the most beautiful locations along the rim unfortunately went into receivership (along with many other developments), instead of being developed to its full potential.

After World War II, a Standard Oil gasoline station, with "modern service bays," replaced Lee's Garage. Paul Stronach owned it for a while. The Bear Fire of the 1950s damaged some of the forest view but did not threaten the restaurant itself. The gas station eventually closed and was torn down, but the Cliffhanger Restaurant continued on, as the view still was fabulous.

During the Panorama Fire in 1980, the Cliffhanger Restaurant was threatened. Firefighters fought the flames that were licking at the building, while evacuated mountain residents watched them battle live on TV. The firefighters successfully kept the fire completely on the south side of the highway and saved the building, too.

In 1981, Cliffhanger Restaurant owner Dino Nanapoulos added 1,500 square feet of space to the old building by adding a duplicate of the original building next to it. The chateau styling with its steep roofline was considered a natural choice, since the structure was near the San Moritz area. The lounge and bar area were expanded, a dance floor was added and the new picture windows in the dining room emphasized the fabulous views of the mountain, forest and valley floor, over 5,000 feet below.

Crestline Resorts and Developments

In the 1990s, a second expansion was designed and built, which included a dining deck and gazebo. Those were added to the eastern edge of the Cliffhanger building. Many couples have been married on the observation deck, backed by the forest, with breathtaking mountain views surrounding them.

When the Old Fire threatened the old wooden building in October 2003, again the firefighters saved the historic 1920s structure from the flames. This time, they sprayed a new gel flame-retardant product on the building and then focused on stopping the furious fire with one-hundred-foot flames from jumping over the highway, which they were using as a firebreak. However, some homes in Arrowhead Highlands burned just a few hundred feet away on the downhill side of Crest Forest Drive.

The Arrowhead Highlands area would probably still be a relatively forgotten area if not for the Old Fire. The 2003 Christmas Day mudslides closed The Narrows between the Crestline Bridge and Crest Forest Drive with resulting months-long detours. Those rains caused parts of the roadway to slip off the southern face of the mountain. It took months for the roadbed to be rebuilt from the canyon depths. That closure sent all the traffic down Crest Forest Drive (initially the route of the Crest Road and then the Rim of the World Road). The drive made by thousands of motorists daily through the middle of the Arrowhead Highlands 1920s subdivision inspired a lot of curiosity about the early days of Arrowhead Highlands and Sphinx Rock, as well as the origins of the Cliffhanger Restaurant.

The filming of *Next*, the Nicholas Cage sci-fi thriller about a man who could see into the future, occurred in 2006 at the Cliffhanger. It saw the construction of two façade buildings in the parking lot (where Lee's Garage had been located) and the use of western décor and covered wagons to create a typical tourist motel. In the story, the motel is located on a cliff with fabulous mountain vistas, exactly like the Cliffhanger's location. The construction of the set at the Cliffhanger slowed Highway 18 traffic as motorists craned their necks to see each new addition as they drove by. During filming of the movie, the entire Narrows stretch of Highway 18 was closed for several weeks, again forcing drivers to detour through Arrowhead Highlands.

The script for *Next* is based on the short story "The Golden Man," written by Philip K. Dick. Ironically, his widow, author Tessa Dick, lives in Crestline. The movie *Next* was released in 2007.

CRESTLINE'S STONE PILLAR: JOHN ADAMS

Crestline has a lot of stone walls, fireplaces, pillars and items made from stone, and John Adams, a true pioneer of Crestline, built many of them from the 1920s to the 1950s. Not only are his rock constructions still standing, but he also made such a difference in the community that some of the traditions and events he began continue today.

Adams arrived in Crestline with his wife, Ida Mae, and their two sons in 1919. That was the same year that S.W. Dillin opened the Crestline Post Office. There wasn't much to see in the uptown area, only Dillin's Tavern and his photography business and stage stop, the post office and a few cabins for vacationing families. It was, at most, a resting place at the crest of the mountain. The Rim of the World Road went directly though Crestline at the time, along what is now Crest Forest Drive. This was before the vacation developers came to the area, and there were fewer than twenty families who lived full time in the mountain area.

John moved to Crestline because he had injured his hand as a mechanic and caught tuberculosis (TB) in the bone of his left hand. The doctor told him to move to a cold climate to thicken up his blood. He opened a mechanic's garage for the Little Bear Lake Company in 1920. He later opened his own garage in Crestline at the 5 Points area, where the road hit the crest (Crestline Cutoff at Crest Forest Drive) when the Mount Andreson Highway to Crestline was constructed. That was a great location for a garage, as many cars needed work after they made it to the crest.

Adams had an engineering degree from Cal Poly San Luis Obispo, where he met his wife. She also earned a degree there, an unusual accomplishment for a woman during that time. Her degree in home economics was just one example of her determination and excellent abilities in many areas.

They brought their two sons with them. The boys loved living in the mountains, fishing in the creeks and hiking through the forest. The oldest son, when he was ten, was kicked in the stomach by a burro. He developed peritonitis, dying tragically two days later. However, this may have motivated John to help the children in the community even more. Over the years, his actions often were dedicated to children.

John Adams was not one to brag, but he was a direct descendant of President John Quincy Adams (and his father, John Adams, the second U.S. president) and felt a responsibility to uphold a good reputation because of those relationships. He lived a long productive life, including paying for three Crestline boys to attend college.

Crestline Resorts and Developments

John and Ida Mae Adams
in 1975, from ROW News.

John and Ida Mae were well-known cooks. For years, Ida Mae cooked for those staying at Camp Seeley. During the Depression years, when the camp was on the American plan, she would prepare meals for up to three hundred campers a day. Her pride and joy were her homemade pies and biscuits.

The Adams family lived in the rock buildings across from Camp Seeley, and in the 1940s and '50s, they ran the Adams Caverns Resort there. The caverns earned the name from the extensive rockwork at the resort. Many of the rock buildings and houses still exist today, built into the hillside like caves but with all the modern amenities of the 1940s, like gas refrigerators and stoves.

In those years, John would cook deep-pit barbecue meat for large gatherings, such as church functions, the Masons or the Fourth of July crowd. Some say that Jamboree Days are a direct result of his annual July Fourth gatherings held at his resort in Valley of Enchantment. He started his annual barbecues in 1945, just after World War II, and they would attract up to seven hundred celebrants. The annual Masonic Deep-Pit Barbecue traces its annual event in Twin Peaks to John Adams, as well. It is said that he built the first deep pit for them to use. These events also led to the awareness of the area and probably, in part, to the influx of new property owners.

Adams made Crestline a better community every time he saw a need. Just after his arrival in 1919, he believed the town needed telephones for residents to communicate with one another and with people in San Bernardino, so he personally walked a wire up the mountain from San Bernardino, attaching it to trees and posts he found along the way. He connected all nineteen families from Twin Peaks to Cedarpines Park on a party line. Ida Mae ran the switchboard from their home. This line was the first network of phones on the mountain. It enabled the families to call for help when they were snowed in, and it became the communication line that made it possible to call San Bernardino for groceries and have them delivered up the mountain by the Mountain Stage Line. This was considered a major upgrade to mountain living at the time.

Back to his excellent rockwork, John used his engineering skills to design and build rock structures all over town. Most early cabins still have his fireplaces warming them. John Adams designed the tall rock walls and steps of the playgrounds at Mary Tone School for the original Crest Forest School in the 1930s. The Civilian Conservation Corps (CCC) did much of the actual work, but under his direction. This saved the school district a lot of money, which was the point of the project. Since they both loved children, he and Ida Mae supported education throughout their lives.

The Switzerland monuments on Lake Drive near Lake Gregory and the San Moritz rock pillar street signs are another excellent example of John Adams's rockwork, which was commissioned as an advertising device by the San Moritz Realty Company to separate itself from any other part of the mountain communities. The Switzerland signs read "Welcome" as you drove eastward past the pillars and "Happy Return" as Club San Moritz members left the club grounds area. These signs were part of the alpine feeling of the Club San Moritz.

John Adams was also the constable for Crestline for several years, maintaining law and order or dragging the disorderly and drunk into Judge Cormack's "courtroom" (in the back room of his real estate office) for sentencing. The job also unofficially involved being sure that the San Bernardino sheriff didn't disturb the bootleggers in the mountain area. I don't want to sully John's reputation, but he admitted to reporter Ken Howell in the 1960s that he drove bootlegged wine and brandy from Cucamonga up the mountain during Prohibition. Since he was a constable at the time, he wasn't suspected, frequently driving up and down the mountain, and he said he never caused a disturbance doing so. He claimed he did it so Ida could use the alcohol for cooking, and he never drank enough to get too drunk.

During the almost sixty years that John and Ida Mae Adams lived in Crestline, they helped shape its growth and added to its personality, built its foundation and helped shaped its future—as true stone pillars of the community, so to speak. John Adams was a fascinating Crestline pioneer and made many positive contributions to the community, both physically and socially.

VI
CRESTLINE
A Vacation Mecca Created by Visionary
Twentieth-Century Pioneers

ARTHUR GREGORY, WHO CHANGED THE
FACE OF CRESTLINE

Arthur Gregory was a Redlands citrus rancher and astute businessman. He came to the San Bernardino Mountain area to set up several small sawmills on tree-covered property he bought in the Crestline area. He planned to produce boxes to transport to market the fruit from his "Pure Gold" brand oranges and other citrus fruit from the packinghouses he owned and operated in Redlands. He found he could save money and have the boxes he wanted when he needed them by having his own sawmills. He purchased several parcels of land from the Arrowhead Reservoir Company.

Gregory and his family enjoyed spending time during the hot summer months away from the sizzling temperatures in Redlands, up under the pine trees in the cooler mountains. He had a summer vacation home in Twin Peaks that he and his family frequented. He supervised his sawmill operations by arriving unannounced.

Gregory purchased Huston Flat and Valley of the Moon from the Arrowhead Reservoir Company when they were liquidating their assets following the 1919 death of James Mooney. He bought the land for the timber it held for his sawmill. He owned the logging rights to Valley of the Moon; he had the valuable timber cut and then subdivided it for recreational use.

He and a partner, A.G. Hamilton, and their wives put the Valley of the Moon development together. A small dam was built across Dart Creek by S. Kenneth Josephs, forming Moon Lake in 1925. That was also the year that a

Arthur Gregory built Lake Gregory.

special part of Gregory's Valley of the Moon subdivision was laid out exclusively for Masons to purchase so they could vacation together in the mountains. They sold the land to other Masons and built a huge resort lodge building, which led to the development of the Arrowhead Valley Club.

Years later, with investors, partially motivated by the drought and seeing a need for a secure water source, Gregory orchestrated the clearing of trees from Huston Flat and having the Civilian Conservation Corps help build a ninety-foot dam across Huston Creek with the intention of flooding the flat to create Lake Gregory in the mid-1930s.

The mid-1930s saw a drought and a Depression, and Gregory knew a lake would provide a steady water source for the growing area and some employment as well. He started the Crest Forest Water District and saw the lake as a recreational tourist attraction. The dam and other facilities of the lake were almost completed when a three-day rain deluge occurred in March 1938, filling the lake in just three days instead of the three years it had been predicted it would take from normal rainfall. The lake was named in his honor.

Gregory owned many other parcels of land, including Thousand Pines Camp, which began because of its location with individual camping sites in the 1890s, and the camp developed over the years into a vacation resort. During the construction of Lake Gregory, the members of the Civilian Conservation Corps who didn't have other homes in the Crestline area stayed at the cabins at Thousand Pines. Gregory donated Thousand Pines to the Baptist Church for a campground and retreat around the time of his death.

Arthur Gregory made a significant impact in changing the face of the western end of the mountain. Those who knew him say there was no one like him, and they will never forget his strong personality that made things happen.

Descendants of his family are still involved with Thousand Pines Camp, which is still operated by the Baptist Church, with Gregory family members having donated a new building to the camp for its seventieth anniversary in 2008. Thousand Pines Conference Center and Retreat offers year-round retreat experiences and an outdoor science camp for youngsters.

CAMP SEELEY, LOS ANGELES SUMMER CAMP

The Valley of Enchantment, a natural bowl in the mountains, with its oaks, cedars and pine trees, has been a prime location for many uses over the years.

First to discover the area were the Indians, who spent thousands of summers there, next to the creek in the beautiful meadow and under the oak trees. Everything they needed for an easy life—pine nuts, water, acorns and small game—was available there. The many arrowheads found there over the years attest to its lure for them. The Indians would move throughout the year from lower elevations to higher ones as the nuts ripened throughout the season. They lived rather peaceful lives, repeating this cycle until Mormon loggers disrupted it in the 1850s.

It was in 1853, after the construction of the Mormon Lumber Road, that early Mormon loggers, brothers David and Wellington Seely, discovered this natural bowl with a creek and chose it as the location of the first water-powered sawmill in the mountains. The mill used the first circular saw in the San Bernardino Mountains. However, the creek proved to be an unreliable power source, so after a few seasons, it was replaced with steam power.

The first Seely Mill was washed out during the Noachian Flood and then rebuilt. The mill site was subsequently sold several times. The area was such a popular location for sawmills because of its location close to the top of the Mormon Road that many other mills opened in the Seely Flat area over the next forty years. Although the numbers of cedar and sugar pine trees were diminished, clear cutting never occurred in the area.

President Benjamin Harrison established the San Bernardino Forest Preserve in 1893. This creation of a protected forest ended many of the lumbering operations in the mountain area. No more lumber tracts were sold, but those that were already privately owned eventually led to land becoming available for homesteading and some limited lumbering.

Around 1900, Judge Byron Waters (Waters Drive is named after him) homesteaded a ranch in the Seely Flat area. He planted apple trees, built a huge barn, fished in the creek and lived there happily until the early 1920s. Then, as he was going blind and couldn't drive the dangerous roads going up the mountain, Waters sold part of his ranch in 1924 to Frank Tetley, who developed it into Rim of the World Park (present-day Valley of Enchantment).

It was 1914 when the City of Los Angeles bought another part of the "Seeley" Flat area as a "Year Round Municipal Mountain Playground." When the City of Los Angeles purchased the land and built the camp, some city administrator "corrected" the spelling of the Seely brothers' last name, and the misspelling has become standard.

The remote campground put Los Angeles on equal footing with New York City in terms of prestige as that eastern city built a network of mountain retreat locations for its residents in upstate New York. Los Angles followed their lead. The San Bernardino Mountains were becoming a popular destination, especially with the opening of the Rim of the World Drive to automobile traffic in 1915, which made accessing the area easier. To reach Camp Seeley in 1916, since most people did not use private cars, could have been very difficult. The dirt roads were steep, with hairpin turns, and it required expert driving skills to negotiate them, so the City of Los Angeles provided transportation to its camp from downtown LA. The campers boarded the Pacific Electric Red Car at Sixth and Main Streets in Los Angeles and would ride in comfort to the end of the line in San Bernardino. There, they transferred to the Mountain Motor Transit Line, a four-cylinder flatbed White truck that had wooden benches bolted onto it (no seatbelts).

White trucks were used for passenger or freight delivery. Mountain Motor Transit ran them on a regular schedule, so the drivers were experienced in driving the narrow dirt road that had few bridges. In 1916, there were still lots of water troughs for the oxen and horses that still used the road.

There were several steep curves, which forced some motorized vehicles to proceed backward up the road to keep the fuel flowing downhill to their engines (because fuel pumps were not invented yet and reverse was the lowest gear for getting up the steep grades, which could be up to 15 percent in some places). This trip usually gave the passengers a real feeling that they were headed into the wilderness, as that trip alone usually gave them enough to write home about, even before they reached Camp Seeley.

When Camp Seeley opened, tent cabins were placed on cement slabs, so it was more upscale than regular tent camping, especially the tent camping

The cabins at Camp Seeley in 1930.

The Lodge at Camp Seeley.

facilities at the Skyland Campground a decade before. Within a few years, twenty-six housekeeping cabins were built. The rustic-style log lodge building was the central meeting place. It had a large fireplace, a stage, a piano and a library for the campers to use. The housekeeping cabins had iron cots and mattresses and were only six dollars a week. They could sleep an entire family, and some had minimal cooking facilities.

A masquerade costume contest was held for the children staying at Camp Seeley in 1922. Lural Mills Schafer shows off her winning costume made from sheets of newspaper.

A swimming pool was added to the facilities in the late 1920s. As the roads to access the mountain area improved, especially with the construction of the High Gear Road between 1929 and 1933, the auto camp became quite popular, costing only fifty cents per car per night, with full use of all amenities, including eating in the dining hall and relaxing and visiting in the lodge with other campers. As the Depression arrived, the many children's activities and seasonal programs made the camp a very attractive place to visit. Few came to visit for less than a full week or two.

Hiking and horseback riding were popular summer activities. The beautiful and nearby Heart Rock Waterfall was a regular destination for the campers. Under the managerial watch of Peter Cormack (later known as Judge Cormack), electricity was installed and the camp flourished.

In the winter of 1930–31, the California Ski Championships were held at Camp Seeley. The ski lift, steel toboggan run and ice rink that were built for the contest were used for several subsequent winters. The camp rented snow play toys to the visitors. After that, the winter snows began lessening in amounts as the drought took hold until there wasn't enough snow to use them. As the 1930s drought progressed, the facilities were dismantled, sold or sent to facilities at higher elevations, and big, organized snow activities ceased.

As the Depression years began, many families spent their entire summers at Camp Seeley to escape the heat of the valley below and enjoy the many activities there. Two popular events were the creative newspaper costume contest and the fishing derby. Kids and adults alike enjoyed the challenge of using only a newspaper to create a costume (worn over their clothes) by folding large pleated collars, skirts and vests from the large pages of the newspaper. Prizes were awarded for the best costume by judges who worked for the camp. One 1921 winner was Mildred Mills, who created a costume making her appear like a Dutch girl. Mildred was the mother of longtime Club San Moritz member and mountain resident Lural Mills Schafer. Her wonderful memories as a child at Camp Seeley made her fall in love with the mountains and encouraged her to move there with her family when she became an adult.

Fishing derbies were also popular. Most of the fish were pulled from Seeley Creek and could be cooked afterward for dinner, whether the fisher was a winner or loser, a true win-win event. One winner didn't even have a fishhook; he just used rocks, a coffee can and fast hands.

Rose and Earl Allen began to manage the camp in 1932 and continued to run it for the next thirty-six years. Natural gas was piped into the camp in the 1940s, replacing the use of propane.

The best-filmed visuals of the camp are in the 1997 Disney remake of the movie *The Parent Trap*. The production company spent the entire summer using Camp Seeley exclusively for the shooting of the movie, which starred Lindsay Lohan as the twin sisters, Natasha Richardson as the mother and Dennis Quaid as the father. The classic log buildings, cabins, lodge, beautiful grounds and Heart Rock hiking trail made it a perfect location for the movie. All the summer camp scenes were shot at Camp Seeley. Many local girls were hired as extras to be the campers in the large group scenes. Many of the other nonspecialized behind-the-scene workers such as production assistants were also hired locally, including Kroft Salmi and David Motley, who had just graduated from Rim of the World High School. Also, the hiking and camping scenes near the end of the movie (doubling as the Sierra Nevadas) were shot at Camp Seeley on the Heart Rock Trail. The lake scenes in the movie are of Lake Gregory.

The night before the Hollywood premiere of *The Parent Trap*, all the girls who were extras had a sneak preview at a special screening held at the Crestline Village Theater.

The City of Los Angeles continues to run the camp into the twenty-first century, and as it approaches its 100th anniversary, Camp Seeley is still in full usage.

ROSE ALLEN, CAMP SEELEY AND CRESTLINE POST OFFICE PIONEER

Many of the women who lived in the mountains in the early days were strong individuals who were involved in creating the character and the inner social structure of the community through the schools, churches and at local post offices. These women, who made a difference in the mountains, include Mary Putnam Henck, Julia Dexter, Pauliena LaFuze, Sara Switzer and Rose Allen, among others.

Rose Allen was active in the Crestline community in numerous ways. She came to Crestline in 1932 when her husband, Earl, was hired to replace Peter Cormack as manager of Camp Seeley. Earl held that position for thirty-six years. The camp, which opened in 1914, is located where the Seely brothers built the first sawmill in the San Bernardino Mountains in the 1850s.

Camp Seeley is owned by the City of Los Angeles, based on a New York City concept that enabled its city residents to experience nature. Even into the twenty-first century, Los Angeles maintains Camp Seeley and sponsors retreats and conferences there.

In the years before the Allens arrived, Camp Seeley became well known because the 1930–31 California Ski Championships and winter carnival held at the camp. During the wet years of the early 1930s, the ski run and toboggan run were actively used.

The first winter the Allens arrived (1932–33), Rose said, was one of the most difficult weather-wise for the area.

"Thank Heaven it was our first year in the mountains," Rose said. "I was young and didn't know what to expect."

The storm came in fast in late December; everything froze very quickly, and then it continued to snow for six more weeks. Seely Flat Road (now Highway 138), which connected Crestline to Valley of Enchantment and Camp Seeley, was closed to vehicle traffic because of the massive amount of snow.

"Early during the storm, the snowplow made one pass at trying to clear the road," explained Allen. "Unfortunately, it broke down, and by the time the needed parts were delivered and installed and it tried to clear the road again, it was impossible to plow because of the depth of the solid ice."

Residents and visitors alike just had to wait until the spring thaw. School was cancelled because no one could get there.

But the city of Los Angeles saw the snow as a new attraction for its mild weather–accustomed city-dwellers and continued sending groups to the campground. Rose continued to welcome them, but with some weather-related modifications. The access solution they devised was a toboggan track through the snow to get food, supplies and propane gas for the camp down from the store located at the crest.

"The campers parked their cars in 'toptown' Crestline and slid down to the camp in toboggans," said Allen. "They considered this a fun experience. The brave camp workers would securely strap supplies to the toboggans, sit on top of the propane bottles and ride them all the way down to the camp. Of course, the campers' return trip to their cars was not as enjoyable. The camp did a good business renting skis, toboggans and sleds that season."

Rose once told me, "That winter was one good memory I'll never forget, but one I also wouldn't like to repeat!"

Rose had one son, Robert, who attended the first through eighth grades at Crest Forest School, located in upper Crestline, later renamed Mary Tone Elementary School, which eventually became the home of Mountain High School until 2010. She organized the first PTA, becoming the first Crest Forest PTA president. The PTA meetings were community get-togethers with dinner inside the school's first building, the cafeteria/gym.

Riding a toboggan was a popular winter pastime, and toboggans were used by Camp Seeley to transport visitors and supplies down to the camp while the roads were closed.

During the mid-1930s, the school was required to have a minimum of seventy students to receive state aid, and Allen worked hard searching for students to enroll to keep those state funds rolling in. Some families were living from spring through fall at Camp Seeley because the Depression had taken their homes. Allen made sure the kids were enrolled in school immediately upon their arrival to keep the enrollment numbers up.

The Allens were charter members of the Crestline Presbyterian Church in 1938, and Rose, along with Mary McBride, started the first Sunday school in Crestline. Most Crestline children attended, as it was both interesting and the only religious education in the area at the time.

During World War II, Rose worked at Norton Air Force Base to help the war effort. The commute was not an easy one, especially in the fog, as the narrow two-lane High Gear Road down the mountain had many twists and curves and was in heavy usage by military buses and vehicles, as Norton AFB rented many vacation cabins in the Crestline area for overflow housing during the war.

Rose recalled one particular 1942 rainstorm when one hundred inches of rain fell and the road washed out in several spots. As she was returning home that night from Norton AFB, the water was so deep in Seeley Creek that had overflowed across the road as she drove down to the camp that it covered the headlights of her car. She was so alarmed that she told Earl as soon as she got home, but he didn't believe her, thinking she had exaggerated the creek's depth. The next morning, he couldn't start the car, so he opened the hood and found gravel on top of the engine block. Earl then said he was amazed the car had even made it back to the camp.

Rose began working at the Crestline Post Office in 1946 and continued there for twenty-two and a half years, until her retirement in 1968, just before Earl retired from managing Camp Seeley in 1969.

During those thirty-six years, Rose Allen saw Crestline grow so much that it outgrew its post office twice. Crestline has never had door-to-door mail delivery, unofficially making the post office the center of most communication, since almost everyone knew everyone else. Getting the mail could take hours because folks would come to pick up their mail and begin talking with their friends, who were also checking their post office boxes. If you wanted to know what was happening in town, the post office was the place to go. Rose once told the Crest Forest Historical Society:

> In those days, when someone came to stay at their cabin in Crestline for the summer, they could get their mail by general delivery, and most who stayed at Camp Seeley did just that. I would suggest it to those who were unaware of that service. If you had friends staying with you, I could write up a card and put it near the boxes and have that mail delivered to your box, so your friends didn't need to stand in line for general delivery. We had a box of cross-referenced index cards on everyone in town. It was quite a convenience for the residents and visitors so everyone could get their mail, even if the post office box number was incorrect or missing, or the letter had a street address, the most common kind of problem. But post office officials won't let the workers do that anymore; they are afraid of the gossip the workers could spread with that kind of information, and made us throw the box away in the late 1970s.

She was a charter member of the Crest Forest Historical Society in 1986 and eagerly shared her stories of the early days of Crestline. She always said she just wanted to make her town a wonderful place to live. Those who knew her believe she succeeded.

PETER CORMACK, CRESTLINE'S JUSTICE OF THE PEACE AND MORE!

Never drink and drive on Crestline's fine roads in the 1920s through the 1950s, or you might spend your night in the back room of Justice Peter Cormack's real estate office—and that was not fun. Judge Cormack did not take kindly to lawbreakers in his town.

Cormack was born in Scotland in 1893. His family immigrated to British Columbia in 1910. He apprenticed himself at age twelve as a cabin boy to a deep-sea fishing boat. He always had high goals for himself.

During World War I, Cormack joined the Royal Air Force and became an aerial gunnery instructor. He was evaluated by his superiors as an excellent pilot and became an instructor. He taught many early aviators, including the first U.S. secretary of defense, Jimmie Forrestal. It was while flying that he got his first informal introduction to Norma Toner, his future wife. While flying his Jenny, he crashed-landed in her father's turnip field. After a formal courtship, Norma and Peter married in 1922 and honeymooned in California, where they spent the rest of their lives.

Cormack first worked for the City of Berkeley as a mechanical foreman. He then studied and was licensed as a doctor of chiropractic. He was interested in many things, including forests and conservation.

He was hired by the City of Los Angeles as the first manager of Camp Seeley to promote recreation and camping. The family moved, in 1926, to Camp Seeley, located next to the new Valley of Enchantment development.

Cormack immediately got involved in the new community, becoming one of the "movers and shakers" of the era. In 1927, he joined the Rim of the World Board of Realtors, staying involved until retiring in 1965.

Peter J. Cormack's most prominent position was as Crestline's local law and order enforcer, as justice of the peace. He was known for his tough sentences for unsafe passing on the narrow dirt roads, drunk driving and later, as the roads were paved in the 1930s, speeding on the mountain roads. Being drunk in public (especially during Prohibition) was a serious offense to Judge Cormack. He had a special room in the back of his real estate office for drunken offenders. He would sentence them the next morning, if they were sober.

After his first appointment as justice of the peace in 1929, Cormack was reelected six more times, until his retirement in 1958 due to health problems.

The West End Rim of the World (ROW) Club was formed in the late 1920s when the various resort owners/managers joined together to advertise, promote and protect the mountain area. Some of the founders, along with Cormack, were Dr. John N. Baylis (Pinecrest), Frank C. Russell (Russell Cabins), Charles S. Mann (Skyland and Crestline subdivisions) and Frank A. Tetley Sr. (Rim of the World Park). With the new High Gear Road under construction, these community promoters wanted "to prove that in these mountains will be found the peak of nature's scenic bounty and recreational facilities," a phrase used in advertising brochures.

One of the ways they wanted to protect the area was shown in their concern over fire. The west enders remembered the destruction of the 1911 and 1922 fires that burned much of Skyland and the Incline Railway. At the urging of the West End ROW Club, the Crest Forest Fire District was formed in 1929.

Dr. Baylis already had his Pinecrest Resort protected by his own fire engine and pump, and he was willing to share them with the community when needed. It was the West End ROW Club's idea that Crestline place fire engines at strategic locations to protect the growing area from uncontrolled fire.

Cormack, as a former Royal Air Force World War II pilot, diligently researched the possibilities of a mountain airport, which he hoped would be located next to Camp Seeley. There was both private and federal forest land adjacent to the camp. It might make access to the mountains easier than the difficult oiled dirt roads that existed at the time. Camp Seeley was also looking for easier access for its visitors. Being in the real estate business, as well, he believed (as most did in that day) that property values would rise if easy access by air were available to the mountain. So Cormack encouraged the club's members, in May 1929, to establish an airport in the Crestline area.

He used his flying connections and brought W.R. Balsom of Western Air Express to speak before the five hundred members and friends of the West End ROW Club:

Access to a territory or community is the pre-dominating factor in determining realty value. Isolated locations…will reduce their isolation. Mountain ranges and steep inclines mean nothing to a high-powered monoplane.

Balsom pitched his idea to the excited West End Rim of the World Club members, who were very interested in the aeroport dream. They wanted to pursue that dream, which never came to fruition because of the stock market crash and subsequent falling property values and foreclosures in

Enjoyment of mountain fun came in many ways at Camp Seeley.

the area. Crestline would have developed very differently with an aeroport within its borders.

Peter Cormack came to Crestline in 1926 to manage Camp Seeley for the City of Los Angeles. He was able to expand the camp and in 1930 added some great winter sports programs and competitions to the recreation programs, on top of the wonderful summer programs. The completion of most of the sections of the High Gear Road to Crestline by 1930 made it possible for vacationers to access the mountains on paved roadways in inclement weather, something not possible previously. In 1930, he organized the first Winter Sports Weekend at Camp Seeley, bringing thousands of tourists to the area. When the Depression arrived, he saw new ways to promote Camp Seeley as a summer retreat from the heat below, advertising that camping was cheaper than staying at other places.

Norma and Peter had two children. They, and others with children, believed a full-time Crestline school was needed. The Crestline area at the time was part of the Summit School District, which had a part-time classroom in Cedarpines Park. Crestline parents wanted their own school. However, it was state policy to only issue approval for new districts with a minimum of seven students. The Crestline School was ready to open on September 1, 1929, as there were eight school-age kids in the area. The parents secured a building on a knoll behind the business district for the school. Then a family with two children moved away, and a problem arose—now there were only six students. What to do? There would be no school for Crestline. Judge Cormack later wrote:

> *Being one of the active proponents of a school in Crestline, I was faced with a dilemma. My daughter, Jeanne, had just turned five and would not be eligible under state law until the second semester of the school year (but if school didn't open that fall there would be nothing for her to attend in the spring). Norma and I were prevailed upon and pressured to allow Jeanne to be enrolled. I don't really know who told the "little white lie," Norma or I, but Jeanne was enrolled and the school opened, in September 1929, with seven students in the house on the knoll above town.*

Jeanne later went on to earn her master's degree at Berkeley, Phi Beta Kappa. Judge Cormack was elected to the Crest Forest School Board and helped start the PTA, along with Rose Allen, eventually becoming a district trustee.

Parent volunteers, coordinated by Cormack, purchased some lots from Crestline developer Charles S. Mann, who also donated adjacent lots for the new Crest Forest School. They built a new twenty- by twenty-foot one-room school building in 1930 on the school site. He was the coordinator of the volunteers when the new two-classroom school building was built in 1932. That site was added on to and evolved over the years from the Crest Forest School into Mary Tone School and, later on, Mountain High School and Mary Tone Educational Center, before closing down in 2010.

The years 1929 and 1930 were big ones for Crestline. Peter J. Cormack, along with the West End Rim of the World Club, was actively jump-starting many clubs and needed services such as the Crest Forest Fire District, the Water District, the Sanitation District and the Crestline Chamber of Commerce. The Lions Club, Crest Forest Women's Club, the Board of Realtors and the Masonic Lodge all have the Cormacks as charter members. Wherever Peter saw a need for the community, he would actively seek a solution.

Another community promotion Cormack was involved in with the chamber of commerce was the "49ers Days at Paradise Gulch" during Labor Day weekend of 1933. It was a community reenactment of Bret Harte's story "The Luck of Roaring Camp." Each community member had a role to play. His character was an immigrant from Scotland, appropriately named "Piper M'Tavish" (because of his accent). The character was described in the newspaper as "having just struck gold in Paradise Gulch...Hoot Mon!"

After the Paradise Gulch riot, the sheriff threatened to throw all the members of the chamber of commerce in jail if any event like that was ever held again, and since Cormack was the secretary of the chamber, it wasn't.

One of the major problems in Crestline, with an increasing population and a drought, was the need for a steady water supply. Many wells were being pumped dry some holiday weekends, which hindered real estate development and sales. Cormack was a driving force in the water district's Lake Committee, suggesting to Redlands citrus grower and sawmill owner Arthur Gregory that there was a great need for a lake in the Crest Forest communities and that his Huston Flat land was the perfect place for it. They convinced him and developer Charles S. Mann that a lake would both supply water and fill a need for recreation for the Crestline community. Gregory agreed, and the land was cleared and a dam was under construction.

When the construction of the dam ran out of WPA funds in 1935, Charles S. Mann withdrew his support for the project. Cormack and Gregory, along with others, organized a letter-writing campaign to raise more money and finish the dam. They finally convinced Charles S. Mann that completion of the lake would be better for his developments than an unfinished, ugly

hole in the ground and got him to join the campaign. Mann even donated money to help finish construction of the dam. Lake Gregory has fulfilled the promise of tourism, recreation and fishing and for many years has provided a steady supply of water to local residents.

Cormack was instrumental in establishing water cisterns to collect water for forest firefighting and the creation of the "skyline firebreaks" to provide firefighters with water in case another fire would dare to threaten the crest communities.

The judge was always doing something or getting involved in many ways to promote the "Crest Forest Township," as the

Judge Peter Cormack.

community was often called in those days. In September 1935, Cormack headed the rodeo committee and helped choose that year's rodeo queen, Helen Stewart, who then represented the Crest Communities in the next rodeo sponsored by the California Highway Patrol, which was then located in Upland.

Daffy, a local dog, brought home a flyer's goggles and belt after an all-day romp in the woods in January 1936. Newspapers reported that Judge Cormack headed a search party for the pilot, who while on a flight from San Francisco to Riverside's March Air Field, may have crashed near Crestline. Cormack was amazingly good at doing things to get publicity for the community and getting his name in the newspaper. He was involved in most of the events of the community as secretary of the chamber. He headed letter-writing campaigns, signed petitions and was very politically involved in the community.

A devastating late November 1938 fire burned the Arrowhead Springs Hotel and threatened Crestline, forcing most of the residents to evacuate. With the completed firebreaks, water cisterns and the Crest Forest Fire Department, along with hundreds of others, they were able to fight the seven-mile-wide fire front and keep the fire out of the tall trees, thus saving Crestline. Some of this was because of the forethought and planning of men like Peter Cormack. The San Bernardino County Board of Supervisors honored him for this and for many other projects in which he became involved.

His knowledge of water, forests and local history helped him convince the county of the need for the San Bernardino County Flood Control District. He received high commendations for all these achievements from the San Bernardino County Board of Supervisors.

During World War II, Cormack, at the age of fifty, enlisted in the California State Guard. He was a relief sergeant in the County Defense Commission. He was to help maintain law and order in the mountain area in case civilian authority was suspended because of civil unrest, air raids or invasion.

Cormack also volunteered to be a member of the United States Selective Service Board and was awarded a Certificate of Appreciation from President Truman. He received a letter from Governor Earl Warren commending his service to the state's civil defense network and promoting him to first lieutenant in the California Guard on September 21, 1950.

It was considered a major local crisis when Walter Winchell, a popular radio and TV commentator, announced in his usual hurried and deliberate delivery style in December 1952 that there was "a communist training school near Crestline, California." Cormack led the protest to Winchell, including sending telegrams, making phone calls, writing newspaper releases and doing newspaper interviews over the charges, which he believed to be untrue.

The San Bernardino County Board of Supervisors supported Cormack's position and issued a January 1953 resolution deploring the "unsubstantiated accusations of Mr. Winchell." Crestline residents were so outraged by Winchell's accusations that the *Crestline Courier* newspaper was printed on pink paper. The community was not open to the idea of communists in their midst.

It was later discovered through testimony at the congressional Un-American Activities Committee meeting that a weekend retreat for socialists may have been held at Camp Tenaya in Crestline. The camp was soon sold.

After winning the 1952 election, Cormack was earning the lowly sum of $157 a month as justice of the peace, which is why he also sold insurance and real estate. His courthouse was the back room of his office, which he provided as a service without compensation.

Governor Earl Warren appointed Cormack to the California Board of Mental Hospitals, and he became active on the board of directors of Patton State Hospital in San Bernardino. He was considered a valuable asset to these boards, despite his Scottish accent.

Judge Cormack didn't run for reelection in 1958 due to poor health and subsequently retired in January 1959. He had served Crestline for twenty-nine years. His gala retirement party was held at Club Oaks in Waterman Canyon, so officials from both San Bernardino and Crestline could easily attend.

It was recommend by his doctor that he live at a lower elevation, so he moved to Redlands. Despite his health problems, Governor Edmond G. Brown appointed him to the State Board of Forestry, with a water emphasis. He created news as articles were written about him after he visited the Pilot Rock area near Cedar Springs, "discussing the state's water concerns." He finally had to retire completely, again due to health problems, but not until 1965, after the decision to create Silverwood Lake was confirmed.

There was a final resolution from the San Bernardino County Board of Supervisors on February 11, 1967, honoring Cormack for his years of service, with the following commendation:

Peter J. Cormack has been a guiding force in the formation of the Crest Forest Fire District, Lake Gregory Water District, Rim of the World School

District, and serving actively in each of these organizations. Cormack has served San Bernardino County well with his 29 years as Justice of the Peace. We recognize Cormack for his instrumental actions in the formation of the San Bernardino County Flood Control District.

The California State Forestry Board recognized Cormack by issuing its condolences upon his death:

Whereas Peter J. Cormack serviced his fellow man in many ways—in the service of his country as a doctor, Jurist, seaman, recreation camp builder and manager, scoutmaster, President and Director of many civic organizations, member of the State Board of Mental Hospitals, member of Boards of Forestry, Flood Control and more, the deep loss of his life will be felt in California for years to come.

The County Board of Supervisors, in its February 20, 1967 resolution recognizing his death, stated in part:

Peter J. Cormack gave unselfishly of his time and talents to numerous civic and service organizations for the betterment of his community; and was loved and respected throughout the county of San Bernardino.

The community of Crestline lost a founding father and creative visionary when Peter J. Cormack died in 1967 at age seventy-three. Judge Peter J. Cormack was single-minded, dedicated and hardworking, with a determination to create a wonderful place to live and visit. The town and community of Crestline would have developed very differently without Cormack's guidance and vision.

BAYLIS OAK TREE

Dr. John N. Baylis has been written about since the day he arrived in San Bernardino as the physician and surgeon for the Atchison, Topeka and Santa Fe Railway in 1887. He was involved in many activities on and off the mountain. He really loved the mountains and especially the trees. It was because of this love that many modern amenities and visitors were brought to the forest.

After being a founder and president of the exclusive Arrowhead Mountain Club at the Squirrel Inn for ten years, Baylis refused an eleventh year. He borrowed money and purchased the 160-acre Smithson Ranch, adjacent to the Squirrel Inn in 1904, instead of allowing the land to be sold to the Guernsey Lumber Mill. Baylis said he couldn't stand the thought of all those old growth trees being cut.

Baylis spent several years developing his Evergreen Village at Pinecrest. He promoted the opening of the mountains to the public while continuing to practice medicine. It was through Baylis's persistence that the county purchased the former logging roads and connected them. The Crest Road, which ran along the mountain top, opened in 1906 for both commercial and privately owned, horse-pulled wagons, making it easier for visitors to visit the forest and the new mountain resorts.

It was in 1909, after sending out ten thousand brochures on the charms of his new resort and promoting the mountains as a vacation destination, that on April 28 he welcomed a trial run of automobiles on the Arrowhead Road through Waterman Canyon and connecting with the Crest Road. He promoted the idea of motorized transportation and then improving the roads for automobiles. The road opened on Wednesdays and Saturdays to autos after May 15 of that year. Baylis held a midnight flag-raising ceremony over his new Pavilion Ballroom as part of the dedication by the San Bernardino Pioneer Society on August 1, 1909. He supported the firefighters during the 1911 fire.

The 1915 dedication of the Rim of the World Road featured a luncheon at Pinecrest honoring Baylis as the originator of the roadway's name after he had widely espoused the beauty of its views for years. The 101-mile-long Rim of the World Road opened motorized access to the mountains. Mountain Auto Stage Line still brought the largest percentage of visitors to the mountains, as only the very rich had private autos at the time. The road allowed both wagon and auto traffic on it for several years.

As the High Gear Road of the Rim of the World Highway, for automobile traffic only, was being constructed up the mountain in the latter 1920s and early 1930s, Dr. Baylis was honored twice for his dedication to the development of the mountains and its roads and his love of trees.

In the 1930s, the High Gear Highway was rerouted to the south slope, eliminating the need for the road to go through Pinecrest's South Park Gate. The Baylis Park Day Use Area overlooking the valley along that new stretch of roadway (now Highway 18) was named in Baylis's honor. The Rim of the World 101-mile historic marker from that 1915 dedication was recently relocated to Baylis Park by the Rim of the World Historical Society since the new road no longer passed its original dedication location.

Crestline

The oak tree that was saved by Dr. John Baylis on Crestline Highway (now Highway 138).

In 1931, after much lobbying by the residents of the Crest Forest area, especially Dr. Baylis, the Crestline Bridge was built off the new High Gear Road. Baylis had pointed out that the original route surveyed called for the destruction of a huge oak tree he referred to as "by far the largest of any to be found on the mountain." Baylis urged that the road be diverted enough "to allow the old tree to continue in its dignity as a chief landmark of the heights." His wishes were respected, and the roadbed was slightly curved around the tree before it entered Crestline.

The Thursday Club, a forerunner of the Crest Forest Women's Club, placed a bronze plaque on the Baylis Oak dedicating the tree to its preserver with a ceremony that honored Baylis and was attended by Crestline's developer, Charles S. Mann, and county supervisor John Andreson Jr. (pronounced ann-Drey-sen), among others. The plaque had been stolen once, but according to news reports, "the thief repented and he returned the plaque to its proper place on the tree."

The tree eventually died and was removed. Its brass plaque was rediscovered just a few years ago and is on display at the Rim of the World Historical Society's Mountain History Museum in Lake Arrowhead.

VII
CRESTLINE GROWS AND DEVELOPS

CHARLES S. MANN: DEVELOPER OF CRESTLINE VILLAGE AND SKYLAND

Charles S. Mann subdivided most of the Skyland and Crestline areas, resulting in his name still being seen on numerous deeds, even today. Prior to his arrival into the mountain area, Mann was referred to as one of Southern California's leading developers in the Los Angeles area.

Through Mann's developments and promotions, the community of Crestline was created. He was the founder of the Rim of the World League, a competitor to the early Crest Forest Chamber of Commerce, promoting real estate and the sale of vacation property instead of businesses. In the early 1920s, Mann and H.A. Ramsey developed the Skyland Heights area next to property being developed by Victor Smith, both adjacent to the former Incline Railroad location. The Incline and other land previously owned by Arrowhead Reservoir Company developer James Mooney was quickly being sold and resold following Mooney's 1919 death.

Skyland had begun as a camping area in the 1890s overlooking the valley below. The Skyland Resort opened in the early 1900s, and some homes were already built in the area, so it was not much of a financial gamble for Mann.

In 1923, Mann also purchased the 430 acres of Guernsey's Crest Resort Property, which at the time was in serious need of attention, between his Skyland and Crestline properties. Mann developed the mountain property "for people of moderate means." In 1928, he bought the town center (donating some land for the Crest Forest School) and remodeled the business

Crestline Grows and Develops

district, constructing the Rim of the World Inn. He used the inn to house prospective property buyers, whom he had bused in from Los Angeles to experience the joys of the mountains and hopefully purchase "a little piece of paradise" for themselves.

Mann promoted the advantages of Crestline in his own monthly newsletter:

> *With the convenience of electricity in Crestline Village and in Skyland, and the daily delivery of gas for heating and cooking, it is no longer necessary to feel that a few days recreation would be spoiled with camp drudgery.*

Mann continued to expand his landholdings, installing roads and utilities as he went. He was quite successful, with over five hundred vacation homes in the Skyland–Crestline Village areas and another thousand nearby resort structures (in other developments) constructed in the vicinity before the Depression began in 1929. He built the Rim of the World Bowl to bring top entertainment to those vacationing in the area. However, bad timing—it opened in the summer of 1929—limited its use and planned expansion of the large amphitheater.

Charles S. Mann was postmaster of the Crestline Post Office, beginning in 1929, after the retirement of Samuel Dillin. He found that being postmaster added nicely to the community and that local residents had to visit the post office frequently; it also promoted his properties. He was able to keep in touch with the pulse of the growing community by being postmaster.

He was not a member of the Crest Forest Chamber of Commerce, and his own competing Rim of the World League often conflicted on the way to properly promote the Crestline area, which was mostly filled with his homes and properties. When the chamber hosted the 1933 Paradise Gulch fiasco, which ended up as a riot of drunken celebrants, he hated the thought so much that he took out an advertisement in the San Bernardino newspaper denouncing the event.

Mann was completely opposed to the construction of Lake Gregory in the mid-1930s, possibly concerned that the lure of the lake would draw interest away from his properties. However, when it appeared the lake project was going to fail and result in a big, ugly, empty hole next to his property, Mann responded to the pleas of local officials, such as justice of the peace Peter Cormack, and donated funds to and supported the completion of Lake Gregory in 1938. The completion of the dam is credited with saving the desert area from suffering extreme flooding after the March 1938 deluge,

This monument honors Crestline's developer, Charles S. Mann.

which inundated much of Southern California and resulted in filling Lake Gregory in three days. The opening of the lake actually did bring new interest to his properties.

However, Mann and Crestline business owners together opposed the building of Lake Gregory Drive connecting with the Rim of the World Road in 1939 at Arrowhead Highlands (the location of the current traffic signal) because that would enable visitors to bypass the town of Crestline when visiting the lake. He was very protective of his town and his own profit potential.

THE RIM OF THE WORLD BOWL: CRESTLINE'S OWN AMPHITHEATER

During the summer of 1930, many activities were encouraging visitors to make the long and difficult trek up the mountain from the sizzling valley below to enjoy the cool, refreshing air during the various events scheduled. The newest amenity for the visitor who craved music and entertainment was the Rim of the World Bowl. The Hollywood Bowl, which opened in 1922, was a great success, inspiring Charles S. Mann.

Rim of the World Bowl was built and owned by Mann, who hoped this would identify his developments as unique and bring culture to his part of the mountain area.

The first season at the Rim of the World Bowl began with its first weekly show on July 18, 1930. The program director was Clyde Garrett, who presented "Symphonies Among the Pines" and "Moonlight Nights of Drama." The bowl was built next to Lake Gregory in a natural amphitheater that, according to Mann, had "perfect natural acoustics."

Visitors from the valley communities were encouraged to come up the mountain and attend the shows and musical performances and then spend the night afterward in one of the many resorts and lodges or in the cabins available for rent.

By 1930, both the Mountain Auto Line (a bus line) and private auto transportation were reliable means of getting to Crestline. The High Gear Road was under construction from San Bernardino to Crestline, with many portions already paved. The newly constructed Bowl Road was designed to create direct access to the amphitheater.

The stage of the Rim of the World Bowl was located near the present corner of Rocky Loop and Forest Shade. There was free parking available for bowl attendees with, as Mann described, "flood lights that have been so placed as to assist the automobile driver in parking his car in the large, free parkway, located only a few steps from the seating area." Mann always described all aspects of his developments in grandiose language.

The thirty-six- by thirty-six-foot stage was built between two stands of "splendid oak trees" and was advertised as "the most beautiful and unique outdoor theater in all of California." It was constructed of solid concrete and was described by Charles S. Mann in brochures about the bowl as "monolithic in construction"; it would last through the ages to "further the artistic and cultural movement that is inspired by the God-given beauty of the Mountains."

An acoustic shell was installed at the back of the stage as a resounding board to give the audience the ability to hear every nuance in the music or voice. "The acoustics are so perfect that the sound of a pin dropped on the cement stage may be heard in the farthest row of seats," boasted the newspaper ads written by Mann.

The stage was "scientifically lighted," with large electric floodlights so it could seem as bright as day on the stage. The lighting could be changed, according to the size of the show, and enhanced the natural beauty of the

The Rim of the World Bowl amphitheater stage at the celebration of the tenth anniversary of Crestline's development by Charles S. Mann.

setting of the bowl. Within the structure, there were dressing rooms and property rooms for scenery and sets. The Rim of the World Bowl was modern in every way.

The seating was also built of reinforced concrete, of an ultra-modern design, built in a great semicircle up the opposite hillside from the stage: "The seating arrangement has been planned so that each spectator commands a full view of the entire stage from any point in the Bowl."

It was hoped the ROW Bowl would expand from the original eight hundred seats to ten thousand seats for future seasons, when needed. Performances were to be presented several times a week during the summer season.

The inaugural program, on July 18, 1930, included an orchestral prelude and an official opening ceremony with dignitaries from the Rim of the World Bowl Association and city officials from several valley cities, as well as officials from the West End Rim of the World Club. Radio station KFXM (San Bernardino) recorded the show for later broadcast. The show featured a chorus of sixty voices, with soloists, and a ballet performance featuring twenty dancers backed by a thirty-piece orchestra.

It was believed the bowl would add greatly to the development of the mountain community. It would add dramatic and musical activities, filling the recognized need for culture and entertainment in the Crest Forest communities and, Mann predicted, would add to property values.

In normal times, the Rim of the World Bowl would have been a huge success, as it was well designed and constructed, with every modern amenity. However, since it opened at the beginning of the Great Depression, it was a financial disaster. It only witnessed a few of the promised "years of quality productions." One of its final big events was the 1933 celebration of the tenth anniversary of the development of Crestline by Charles S. Mann. It silently sat out the rest of the Depression. The bowl deteriorated, was dismantled and has totally disappeared from the Crestline landscape.

SNOW PROMPTS REALIGNMENT OF RIM ROAD

Snowstorms are what prompted the realignment of Rim of the World High Gear Road to the south face of the mountain when it was constructed in the late 1920s to mid-1930s. It was built there to allow the snow to melt in sunlight, instead of being clogged with ice and snow for weeks on end or requiring the use of expensive snow-removal equipment.

It's important to remember that private ownership of autos in the mid-1920s was still a relatively new concept, as automobiles had only been commonplace for about fifteen to twenty years. The original dirt surface of the Rim of the World Road had opened to automobile traffic in 1915. Much of that route had been the reworked 1911 Crest Road, which had been created from the old lumber roads the county had purchased around 1905. The 1915 road had been oiled to keep down the dust. That oiled surface was considered to be "high tech" when it was applied.

The concept of a self-melting, south-facing paved road sounded even better, and it would work well, since the typical weather pattern after small snowfall amounts in the San Bernardino Mountains is often characterized by days of warmer weather and sunshine. In those early days, the few people living on the mountain would just stay home for a few days until the roads cleared or get out their shovels if they needed to go somewhere. It was rare for a person to drive the road up and down the mountain daily.

The oil-covered dirt 1915 Rim of the World Road was realigned in many places along the rim with the construction of the paved High Gear Road. It was going to be an entirely new route into the mountains, designed for the new mode of transportation: automobiles. The realignments were necessary for widening the road to two lanes so cars could pass going in opposite directions at any spot. Reducing the grade to only 6 to 8 percent was essential so cars could travel uphill in high gear, which is why it was called the High Gear Road. This is what led to the word "highway." The realignment also eliminated many sharp hairpin curves. With the completion of the High Gear Road, no driver was forced to drive around a sharp, steep curve in reverse any longer to get up the roadway, as had been the norm at spots along the original 1911 Crest Road and even in some spots on the original 1915 Rim of the World Road.

Instead of having the road routed along the bottom of Waterman Canyon, the first place it was relocated was a "cut-in" halfway up the west canyon wall above Waterman Canyon, bypassing the canyon floor completely. This was because the lower road was prone to flooding. That west canyon wall route was widened later in the 1960s with the cantilevered bridges becoming what is today Highway 18.

The second place where the road was significantly realigned was just past the large, almost 340-degree curve where the Caltrans maintenance station was located at Panorama Point. That old highway repair station, built during construction of the High Gear Road, burned during the 2003 Old Fire and has since been removed, but the large curve is still there.

Crestline Grows and Develops

Prior to the construction of the High Gear Road, the old route of the Rim of the World Road, with its thirteen switchbacks, climbed the steep southern face of the mountain, leaving the current route just past Panorama Point, west of Bonnie Wee Canyon, and reached the rim near where St. Francis X. Cabrini Catholic Church is now located. As the 1915 Rim of the World Road, it ran along the route of Crest Forest Drive through uptown Crestline and continued eastward to Arrowhead Highlands. There the road traveled past the Squirrel Inn (the current route of Highway 189) to Pinecrest. Then the road went through the Pinecrest stone pillars on the right side of the current road and over the crest to the south of Strawberry Peak, where it turned and went out to the rim again, just west of Rimforest.

The southern-face cuts for the new mid-1920s automobile route started at Panorama Point and continued eastward along the south face with a bridge over Bonnie Wee Canyon toward where the Crestline bridge is located and then below Skyland. This kept the roadbed at a lower elevation, as well as on the south face for the snowmelt.

The new road access to Crestline, recommended by the Crest Forest Chamber of Commerce, cut off the new highway just west of Skyland at the point where the Incline Railway crossed the new route. To keep it at less than an 8 percent grade, it needed the bridge. This is now the route of Highway 138. County supervisor John Andreson Jr. got this direct route to Crestline funded and constructed.

The High Gear Road was cut into the granite across the steep, almost eighty-degree south face of the mountain from Incline Point to Arrowhead Highlands, which was considered a great engineering feat. This is now considered The Narrows of Highway 18 between the Crestline Bridge and the Cliffhanger in Arrowhead Highlands. The engineers at the time were unaware of the massive earthquake fault that runs through that area, which frequently causes rocks to rain down on the highway, even today, or they may not have chosen that route.

The High Gear Road then continued across the south face past where Baylis Park is now located and connected to the old road west of Rimforest.

The construction of the High Gear Road greatly changed the mountains. It made access to the mountains and Crestline easier. The stage/bus lines and autos could now get up the mountain with greater ease on the two-lane highway, as inventors improved the vehicles' mechanics as well.

The developers who were selling resort property all over the mountain knew the High Gear Road would bring more customers and vacationers and change the mountain into communities and towns. And Crestline would

Crestline in the 1930s, after the fire station and post office relocated.

have grown sooner than it did if the Great Depression and World War II hadn't hit. But having a road designed and already under construction gave those in the Civilian Conservation Corps (CCC) and the Works Progress Administration (WPA) during the Depression "shovel-ready jobs" and introduced them to the mountain. Many of the workers returned after World War II to purchase vacation homes.

The roads to the mountains have changed over the years, from logging roads so steep that a log had to be dragged behind the wagon to keep it from running over the oxen to today's four-lane highway, where CHP officers have to remind drivers of easily maneuvered cars of the speed limits, both going up and down the road. What was at one time a seven-plus-hour journey to Crestline by horse- or oxen-pulled wagon is now a quick fifteen-minute car drive up or down a freeway. What a change!

CRESTLINE: EARLY 1930S

As the Depression and dustbowl conditions swirled around America's Heartland, Crestline continued to grow. The road up the mountain had just been improved, and the automobile made access quicker and easier than the horse-drawn buggies had been. People could now travel up to twenty-five miles per hour on some of the newly paved stretches of the High Gear Road.

Yes, there were many who were out of work in California, and a few of the recent mountain subdivisions, without sufficient financial backing, did go bankrupt; some of those out of work people did allow the state to take their lots for unpaid taxes. However, because the area was "new" (meaning most people had owned their properties less than five years), not a lot of great value was lost, since most lots had been sold for amounts in the low hundreds and on time payments.

Camp Seeley had public camping sites, and many families went there to live all summer during the Depression years. It was cheap, had a full kitchen that served meals and had a lovely climate. They had activities for the children, and if a husband was working for the Civilian Conservation Corps, this was a safe place for his family, especially if the family was "between homes."

From 1923, when the community began, to 1935, growth had been slow but constant in the Crest Forest area. The Crest Forest area at the time consisted of Valley of the Moon, Cedarpines Park, Pine Crest Resort, Arrowhead Highlands, Skyland, Rim of the World Park (now Valley of Enchantment), Dart Canyon, Valley View, Clifton Heights, Horseshoe Bend, Arrowhead Highlands and the Crestline subdivision. Over 650 homes had been built, and the community had a population of over one thousand. The apple ranchers who had homesteaded the Dart Canyon area kept their land parcels intact.

In 1935, Crestline had "more registered voters than any other unincorporated area in California, not adjacent to an incorporated city," according to the *San Bernardino Daily Sun* newspaper. In fact, since the Depression began in 1930, over 200 new homes had been built, and they expected another 170 to be finished by the end of 1936, said the article.

The Crestline Bowl, a new amphitheater built by Charles S. Mann, was complete and ready for use. It had excellent acoustics, was wired for electric lights and had seating for hundreds and room for expansion and hillside picnicking.

All the Crest Forest organizations were growing. The Crest Forest Fire Department was established in 1929, and by the mid-1930s it had ten well-trained volunteer firemen, with three fire station locations, each equipped with a truck. The district had an assessed valuation of $986,000.

The Crest Forest Real Estate Board just kept selling property, and the Crest Forest Chamber of Commerce was actively promoting the area. The Crest Forest Justice Court, under Judge Cormack, was active.

The Crest Forest School, which opened in 1929, was also growing, now serving seventy students in grades one through eight. Crestline had another twenty students who were attending high school in San Bernardino. Many of those students stayed the weekdays down the mountain with families and would return to their own families during the weekends because of the amount of time it took to drive up or down the High Gear Road.

The current-day Olde Town Crestline business district looks very similar today as it did then, as it still has most of the same buildings. However, it had many more businesses back then, with a hotel; a gasoline station; hardware, drug and grocery stores; and restaurants, as well as real estate and insurance offices and two parks.

Crestline had the largest number of electrically connected houses in the mountain area and the highest number of phone connections, too. Yes, Crestline had everything a growing mountain town needed to face a prosperous future in the 1930s. It wasn't Crestline's fault that the stock market fell and the economy went sour; the town was prepared to grow.

PARADISE GULCH

In September 1933, the Crest Forest Chamber of Commerce decided to put on its fourth-annual "49er Days." During the previous three years, the festivities had been designed with the intention of bringing visitors, with their money, up from the flatlands to party in the beautiful forest and pine-scented mountain air, spending as much of that money in the mountains as possible.

The successful 1932 event had taken place at Thousand Pines Camp, an old location that had been used as a resort after it closed its lumber mill operations in the 1890s. The Crest Forest Chamber of Commerce renamed the resort Lucky Strike for that weekend, which included some gambling, dancing and various amusements. The 1931 49er Days had been called "Bloody Hollow," renamed after another infamous old gold rush town, so everyone knew what to expect and was excited about the huge end-of-the-season mountain event. For 1933, 49er Days was expanded and relocated to Valley of the Moon, closer to Twin Peaks, because it was to be bigger and better than the previous three events.

Valley of the Moon had been the location of the Arrowhead Valley Club before the Depression. It had a shallow lake, the large rustic log clubhouse and a town square, excellent for setting up a boxing ring and for dancing. It had room for booths, a sixty-foot bar and a sideshow. It was two and a half miles away from Crestline and about the same distance down from Twin Peaks, a centralized Crest Forest location, described in the advertisements as "a charming spot in the mountains, rugged pine tree covered slopes all about, a tiny lake in the center— is the site of a perfect Paradise Gulch for 49er Days."

The concept was to re-create an 1849 gold rush town for visitors to experience. It was based on the Bret Harte short story "The Luck of Roaring Camp." The citizens of Crestline each had a character from the town of Paradise Gulch to portray. The visitors could then come mingle and experience what life was like during the gold rush era. The pine-mountain environment added to the gold rush town atmosphere. Harte's story was printed in the *Paradise Gulch Era* newspaper so everyone would know it:

> *This is your gold camp, built for your pleasure; for your happiness and joy and laughter. This year, it is the biggest thing ever attempted for it combines all the features of a carnival, mid-way, fiesta, gold camp and gala holiday. This year's carnival will be the last word in 49ers. It will pass before your eyes as a great play of color, gaiety and enchantment. A play in which you, whether you come in costume or not, will be one of the actors. A play of milling pleasure seeking people leaving their cares and worries behind them to rub elbows with those in Paradise Gulch 84 years ago on the slopes of the High Sierras.*

49er Days was promoted all summer long as a family outing to celebrate the end of the summer. Because the era they were re-creating was eighty-four years before 1933, everyone was encouraged to wear period costumes, and some of the advertising even suggested where to rent the costumes. United Costumers, Inc., of Hollywood brought its costume racks to the Fuller Paint Company annex at 395 E Street in San Bernardino to give down-the-hill residents the opportunity to get historically accurate clothing for the weekend event.

The advertisements in the newspapers and on the radio were everywhere. Crestline even printed its own eight-page newspaper for the event, the *Paradise Gulch Era*, which was passed out all over the county prior to the weekend. The headline announced: "Mountains Will Rock with Revelry Sept. 16!"

Paradise Gulch was described:

> *It will pass before your eyes as a great play of color and gaiety and enchantment. A play of milling pleasures, seeking people, leaving their cares and worries behind them to rub elbows with bearded miner, soldier, sailor, bad man, lovely lady, just as they appeared in the old Paradise Gulch. And all under the spell of a warm pine scented mountain night... This great*

carnival will turn back the hands of time for a day. We want you to re-live in reality the days of gold that meant to all the building of California. Again, the Town Square will ring to the shouts of happy miners. Again, the dance hall will rock and thunder to the time of happy dancing feet as strains of yesteryear pour forth their sweet melodies to eager ears. Just two and half miles from Crestline will be a living, breathing replica of the feverish gold days that marked the winning of the West.

After reading such colorful descriptive language, who wouldn't be excited about attending the event? The weekend had activities planned for all ages. For the twenty-cent entry fee, there was the McKenzie Show for the kids in the big tent. There was ice cream, soda, candy and '"side show marvels" for only a dime more: "Old time side shows will fling their colored banners to the four winds as husky-voiced barkers tell of fire eaters, two-headed women, sword swallowers, hula girls and many other attractions."

There was one significant difference between Paradise Gulch and the three previous gold rush town re-creations: Prohibition was over! Beer would be flowing freely, definitely a new attraction from the previous three events:

The music of tinkling glasses will be heard along the sixty-foot-long bar. And, as a final touch, true to the traditions of the old west will be present in the form of the Maier Brewing Co. and the master beer that has quickly earned the appreciation of connoisseurs of fine brew since the end of Prohibition.

Everyone knew that in the saloon, gambling was a fun pastime, so they advertised:

Row after row of splendid gaming tables offer all and sundry to tempt the goddess of chance. Blackjack, chuck-a-luck, craps, stud poker, and, new to most of us, that dazzling of all games, Tango. All will be there, set in an atmosphere most akin to the old gold rush days, when lucky miners, clerks, teamsters and gamblers...called to chance to make their winnings great.

The newspaper headline proclaimed, "Crest Foresters Put Shoulders to Wheel to Make Paradise Gulch Gold Town Dazzling Success." The weekend of September 16, 1933, was about to make Crestline well known.

Townsfolk from all over the mountain adopted character personalities from the story to create the feeling of an authentic 49er gold rush town.

Rough Garlick

—Slings world champion hamburgers at the "Red Onion" — eatin' place of the Bright Angel Bar. GIVE MINE THE WORKS, BO. ..

This, of course, is JOHNNY ADAMS who, with Mrs. Adams, maintains the delightful Adams Inn just outside Rim O' the World Park

Steam Beer Andy

—Looks a bit pale in the gills under the derisive laughter of one neighbor and the thought of what's going to be done to him by the other!

But just the same he's FRANK C. RUSSELL, most cheerio guy in the mountains, president of the chamber of commerce, Big Crestline Hardware & Resort Man.

Goose Oil Doolittle

—IS the high priest of pills and castor in Paradise Gulch! No one ever sees Doc's mistakes BECAUSE HE BURIES THEM ALL. . . .

Really this is A. C. McCardle, the popular Crestline barber. So far as the records go he's never yet slit a throat or drawn FIRST BLOOD. . . .

Newspaper ads were run for Paradise Gulch, with John Adams for Adams Caverns, chamber of commerce president Frank Russell and A.C. McCorde, Crestline's barber.

They chose a character either based on their ethnic heritage or completely opposite of themselves.

San Bernardino County supervisor John Andresen Jr. came up the mountain to portray the character Commodore Robert Stockton, a real-life personality who commanded the American Squadron, which took California.

Lake Arrowhead sawmill owner John Dexter was Rifle Ball Grogan (sheriff of Placer County). At least fifty characters were listed in the newspaper, all with creative descriptions.

For example, Crestline's large landowner Beth Cathcart was "Lady Wanda from Kilbraikie Castle"; Hal Davies (later a local sheriff) played "Mule Hide Ben," a mule skinner who bucks the tiger; Judge Peter Cormack portrayed "Piper M'Tavish," a corporal in the Scottish Highland Regiment, now scrambling for gold in Paradise Gulch; and volunteer fire captain and businessman Frank Nardi adopted the character of "Jim, the Pen Man," who left Sing Sing just in the nick of time. Community members were looking forward to a fun-filled weekend re-creating the Old West.

Most every business or organization on the mountain either sponsored a concession stand or a character. There were twenty open-air booths with raffles and games. About 1,500 visitors were expected, which was quite a large crowd for the Depression.

Even businesses in San Bernardino were involved, mostly for the advertising they got in the newspaper/playbill when the characters were described, sponsoring ads on KFXM radio.

"Personal motor cars" from San Bernardino were to drive

> *up Waterman Canyon to the High Gear Road, to Crestline. Then it is two-miles of easy paved roads to parking in Houston Flat—then motor transit busses will take visitors the half-mile over the hill to Paradise Gulch. Or Pacific Electric Motor Transit stages is offering excursions from any Southern California point directly to the gold town.*

To maintain the 1849 feeling, all cars were banished from the Valley of the Moon and given free parking in Huston Flats, away from view (it was 1933, and Lake Gregory was not built until 1938).

Mountain Transit buses and "Faire Cars" were also making round trips from San Bernardino to bring up visitors. The Faire Cars claimed they could make the trip from downtown San Bernardino in less than one hour.

The adult entry fee to Paradise Gulch was fifty cents. The Crestline Chamber of Commerce ran a script exchange booth at the entrance to discourage pickpockets and other cash-related problems. (The script was issued by the Snow Bank.) Every need of the visitor, whether it was food, beverage, gambling, entertainment or dancing, was available for the script.

The event began at 2:00 p.m., enabling Crestline restaurants to serve breakfast or lunch to those who arrived early, intending to escape the sizzling heat of the valley below.

During the afternoon family hours, the bar was closed, but the bands were playing for dancing and entertainment. The McKenzie Players, a professional sideshow, had been invited to perform for the youngsters, advertising "Violet the half-lady, Floretta the two-headed girl, Vulcan eats fire; Amazu the Mystery reads minds and Lucretia Borgia in a pit with pythons."

The evening events were designed for more mature interests. Some of the entertainment included live orchestras such as the Cherokee Bandits,

The boxing match between CCC Camps at Paradise Gulch.

Ossie's Band and Borrell's Fine Band, all "keeping the Dance Floor in motion from 2 PM on into the night." There was a sixty-foot-long bar and various card games of chance (almost real gambling, legal only because they were using script). Free hourly in the Town Square was live entertainment such as hula dancers.

The top events were the boxing matches arranged between rival Civilian Conservation Corps (CCC) camps. Saturday evening's 10:30 p.m. featured event was two four-round boxing matches. The regulation-sized raised platform was constructed in the town square, and the boxers used four-ounce gloves.

The competitors were volunteers from the Santa Ana Canyon Camp #511 that put forth Harry Hodge at 158 pounds and James Horton at 138 pounds against the boys from Miller Canyon #542 (the canyon now flooded by Silverwood Lake), Oliver Thomas at 160 pounds and General Lawrence at 138 pounds. The fights themselves went without a hitch. The mostly male crowds loved the competition and were enthusiastically yelling for their favorites.

A few days later, in the *San Bernardino Sun* newspaper, Charles S. Mann, promoter of the Crestline Village subdivision, paid for this display ad:

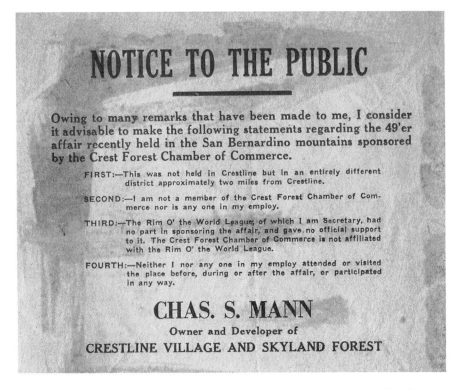

NOTICE TO THE PUBLIC

Owing to many remarks that have been made to me, I consider it advisable to make the following statements regarding the 49'er affair recently held in the San Bernardino mountains sponsored by the Crest Forest Chamber of Commerce.

FIRST:—This was not held in Crestline but in an entirely different district approximately two miles from Crestline.

SECOND:—I am not a member of the Crest Forest Chamber of Commerce nor is any one in my employ.

THIRD:—The Rim O' the World League, of which I am Secretary, had no part in sponsoring the affair, and gave no official support to it. The Crest Forest Chamber of Commerce is not affiliated with the Rim O' the World League.

FOURTH:—Neither I nor any one in my employ attended or visited the place before, during or after the affair, or participated in any way.

CHAS. S. MANN
Owner and Developer of
CRESTLINE VILLAGE AND SKYLAND FOREST

This newspaper notice from Charles S. Mann denied responsibility for the Paradise Gulch riot.

One thing about Charles S. Mann—he always let others know exactly where he stood.

This is how it all went down:

After the boxing matches that hot September evening, a fight broke out among the approximately two thousand viewers in attendance (one-third more than anticipated), as some (possibly from the CCC camps) did not like the refereeing. So some of the bystanders attempted to separate those disagreeable drunk souls, turning the festivities into a mêlée and near riot. Men were piled on top of one another with fists flailing. There were more getting hurt around the ring than got hurt during the fights. The women ran away in fright, and fortunately, the children had all gone home hours before.

The single constable had no way of separating the fighters from those trying to stop the fight and still protect the innocent bystanders. So, in desperation, he ran to the electric power switch and threw the entire festival into total darkness.

Most of the fighters cooled down in the darkness. Those who didn't were knocked out cold by the constable if they wouldn't listen to reason, threats or anything else. When the lights were restored, it was discovered that not only had fighting ensued but also the booths had been looted, including one booth that lost twenty hams intended to be raffle prizes.

Doc White showed up (no one was sure if he was a real doctor) and stitched up the injured before they were sent home.

The constable was quoted afterward as saying he would "refuse to ever have such an event scheduled during my tenure again." County sheriff Emmet Shay said if anything like 49er Days ever happened again he would "lock up the whole committee" who organized it. Those who had been against the repeal of Prohibition had another example of the evils of booze and gambling.

And nothing called, or anything that resembled, 49er Days has ever again been staged anywhere near the San Bernardino Mountains since that day.

VIII
LAKE GREGORY ERA

BUILDING LAKE GREGORY

A Lake for Crestline

In the mid-1930s, Crestline was beginning to grow, and small struggling businesses were beginning to fulfill the needs of the many visitors and residents. There were two competing civic groups promoting the area: the Rim of the World League, headed by Charles S. Mann (developer of the Crestline subdivisions), and the Crestline Chamber of Commerce, with Judge Peter J. Cormack as its secretary. Both groups wanted to find a way to create tourism and encourage growth in the various subdivisions. They were envious of the number of tourists who flocked to enjoy Lake Arrowhead.

In 1934, the Depression forced some of the subdivisions into bankruptcy, and approximately 22 to 39 percent of the properties were tax delinquent. Bad publicity from September's brawl during 49er Days at Paradise Gulch had sullied the chamber of commerce's image.

Many displaced families were living at Camp Seeley during the warmer months. They could live cheaply, since the camp was on the American plan of rates including meals. Besides, the weather was so nice in the mountains during hot summer months.

The Crest Forest School District wanted to improve the school and provide jobs for the unemployed. The school board requested Civil Works Administration (CWA) and State Emergency Relief Administration (ERA) funding to develop the school grounds and provide work. These resources created the beautiful rock walls, tennis courts and field with the district paying only a small percentage for the cost of materials. Rocks were cheap, local and plentiful, and engineer/wall builder John Adams was supervising. There was also a growing concern over reliable water sources for the communities. With a growing population and drought years, some water wells were pumping dry. Large landholder Arthur Gregory, who owned Thousand Pines Camp and had developed Valley of the Moon, had also, in 1926, bought Huston Flats, where he was operating a small sawmill making boxes for the oranges he grew in Redlands.

Gregory suggested reviving Charles S. Mann's five-year-old proposal of building a seventy-foot-tall dam across Huston Creek at Miller Canyon (an area that Gregory owned) and creating a lake. Gregory proposed creating and then heading the Crest Forest Water District to operate the lake. Landowner Bess Cathcart also volunteered to donate part of her ranch to be the lake. Between them, over eighty acres of land were donated to create the lake. It was believed a lake would provide water and raise tourism and property values, too.

It was through Gregory's efforts that the Crest Forest Water District was formed and that the Work Project Administration (WPA) was persuaded to build a dam to conserve the natural water of the area for the use of the local people. The WPA employed local men who had just finished the work on the school ground walls to build the dam and prepare Huston Flat for a lake. The town would receive a reliable source of water for the growing subdivisions and a lake to promote tourism, too. Property development and water conservation were two of the goals for the WPA.

The proposed cost of the dam would be low, as most of the expense would be in labor. The WPA proposed hiring fifty to one hundred men at a time during various stages of building the dam to speed the project on its swift timetable. The initial estimate was $80,000 to $100,000 for the entire project. The water district issued a twenty-year bond for the amount of $25,000, and Arthur Gregory contributed $5,000, while Charles S. Mann donated $2,500. The WPA would foot 80 percent of the cost and supply the equipment.

The Rising Costs of Building a Lake during the Depression

Arthur Gregory formed the Crest Forest Water District to finance the lake. The tax bond would tax property owners at the rate of 6 percent per $100.00 of assessed valuation of property for building the dam and lake. In 1935, most Crestline lots cost $50.00, and the average taxable value of a lot and cabin was $250.00. So, this meant a tax increase of $0.75 per year. Over the twenty years, the tax bond would add $15.00 in taxes.

The dam/lake project began in July 1935 and was scheduled for completion in 1937. The dam would be four hundred feet long across Miller Canyon, with a compacted lake floor.

Richard Tetley of Valley of Enchantment remembered how strange it was to visualize how high up the hillside the water would reach from his perspective on the floor of Huston Flat, now the lake's bottom. Another teenager at the time, Ruth Harper, whose cabin was on Old Mill Road, remembers the loud steam shovel engines and tractors echoing around the previously quiet valley that summer.

The first step in the project was hiring the fifty to one hundred men for the removal of brush and trees. The trees were used by Gregory's sawmill to make his orange-packing crates. The water district drilled a five-hundred-foot-long diversionary tunnel, four by six feet tall, through solid granite, and it needed to be lined with concrete. It would take one hundred men four months to complete the tree and tunnel projects.

Construction of the Lake Gregory dam.

Next, a temporary dam was built to divert the water from the twelve local streams to flow through the tunnel. Over 17,500 yards of decomposed granite had to be excavated down to bedrock. The soil quality was excellent for an earthen dam. The moisture content of the soil was tested daily: too wet and the mud would clog the rollers in the compacting equipment; too dry and soil compacted poorly. The dam's core was clay from nearby clay beds.

Due to foundation problems and increased excavation and fill work, the project went 46 percent over its $100,000 budget. Also, heavy snows in 1936 raised the cost. Additional funding approval from WPA was delayed, stopping work and sending all 350 workers to other projects. Another $16,000 was required immediately from the local water district for its 20 percent share of the cost.

It was at this time that Charles S. Mann withdrew his support for the dam project for being "too expensive." During the 1937 summer, Huston Flat was turned into an unfinished dam and a giant eyesore of a hole, devoid of trees. The community quickly banded together at the gentle persuasion of Gregory, Judge P.J. Cormack and others, who raised the funds to complete the dam through donations and the selling of construction bonds. Eventually, C.S. Mann promised a donation of another $2,500 upon completion.

When funds were guaranteed from both the water district and the WPA, a new work crew was hired, and the work was resumed. With the January 1938 deadline approaching, the final packing of 100,000 cubic yards of earth for the dam, plugging the diversion tunnel and the final completion of the spillway needed to be completed. The spillway would be an emergency outlet if the water level ever approached the top of the dam.

The Dam Is Completed, the Lake Fills

The January 1938 completion deadline was not met, but it was close enough that (WPA) funding was not cancelled. By the end of February, the lake/dam was 95 percent completed. The future lake floor was still being compacted, and the diversionary tunnel was blocked, so some water (about five acre feet) was being stored. It was predicted that it would take three to five years to fill the lake.

To get permission to build the dam/lake, written approval was obtained from farmers and landowners downstream. In return, the Las Flores Ranch was promised an amount of water each season and protection from flood damage.

Compacting is performed at the dam (the part that, as this book goes to press, needs repair).

In March 1938, it began to rain and rain. The area got thirty-four and a half inches of rain in seventy-two hours! The sixteen springs and creeks became raging rivers and flowed into the lake basin. This was actually good; otherwise, the water would have naturally converged in the canyon and roared down the mountain toward the community of Cedar Springs. The dam, although not 100 percent finished, held, thus averting downstream disaster. The lake filled quickly.

John Adams said he and others were called upon to get the steam shovels and other heavy equipment out of the lake basin before it completely flooded. Adams said, in 1975, "We succeeded, but there was still some equipment left that we couldn't get out in time." He believed winches dragged up most of the equipment later, as it was too valuable to leave there.

The city of Los Angeles was flooding, and the Santa Ana River was devastating Orange County. Lake Gregory filled in three days, saving downstream properties from similar destruction. The water flowing over the spillway saved the dam from flood damage. However, the road at the spillway was washed away.

After the storm, water was released from the lake to repair the road and spillway and finish installing the rock face on the dam. All was completed by the summer.

By the summer of 1938, large feature newspaper articles, with maps and pictures, marveled about the pristine beauty of the new Lake Gregory, encouraging people to come visit. A ten-cent fee was collected to keep the area clean and sanitary and to build facilities at the lake. Lake Gregory had two and a half miles of shoreline, a surface area of 126 acres and a depth of 95 feet and stored 2,580 acre feet of water. Stream fishing had always been popular in Crestline. Rowboats were almost immediately launched during fishing season onto the new lake.

The lake was named for Arthur Gregory, who created the Crest Forest Water Agency, donated the land for the dam and spearheaded the project to completion through various difficulties. He even loaned an extra $60,000 when the project was stalled, encouraging others to invest. Had he not done this, the water district would have failed, and the flood would have washed away the uncompleted dam, causing downstream destruction and financial losses.

After the proposed Lake Gregory subdivision agreed to donate a one-hundred-foot-wide strip of land to the county for a road from Arrowhead Highlands to the lake, its subdivision plans were approved. The board of supervisors approved creating Lake Gregory Drive, budgeting for prison laborers to do the work.

Controversy immediately arose over the road's construction. The Crestline Village Businessmen's Association did not want Lake Gregory Drive built, as visitors might bypass Crestline. They wanted their tax dollars spent realigning the existing road, not creating a new one. The businessmen agreed that the procurement of an easement through the new subdivision would be wise but said, "A road at this time is unnecessary."

In 1940, after a special audit of the Crest Forest Water District, Arthur Gregory, its president, asked whether the $60,000 loan he made to complete the dam could be repaid to him. Legally, no officer of a public district was allowed to be a party to a contract involving loans. Gregory did it because the district couldn't obtain the necessary funds elsewhere.

When all was resolved, seventy-year-old Arthur Gregory was given this tribute:

Notwithstanding the irregularities in procedure and notwithstanding the apparent personal interests involved, the creation of Lake Gregory has furnished the San Bernardino mountain area with a desirable lake and future water supply. It is our opinion the present dam could not have been completed without the efforts and cash advances from Arthur Gregory. Doubtless, Mr. Gregory spent much time and considerable money for which no reimbursement has been made in his efforts to complete the dam and lake.

Fun is the operative word at Lake Gregory.

Bess Cathcart, one of the lake development supporters who donated 70 acres under the new lake, sued Arthur Gregory in 1940 over receiving clear title to her land surrounding the lake. The lake was to have 175 feet around the shoreline dedicated to the public domain, and that was in debate, as was the $10,000 she had borrowed from Gregory in 1926 and not repaid. She sued to prevent foreclosure on her 225 acres of land around the lake, as its value had now greatly increased.

The subdivision by the Lake Gregory Land and Water Co. also proposed constructing a village consisting of new homes and businesses in the new Lake District. The Crestline businessmen were not happy with that idea, either. But after the dedication of the easement and agreeing that all roads in the subdivision would meet county guidelines and be dedicated as county roads, the county quickly granted approval for the new subdivision.

There was no sand at the beach, so in the early 1950s, sand from the riverbed of the Santa Ana River was trucked up the mountain and spread over the west end of the shoreline.

In 1951, the exclusive Club San Moritz moved from the Valley of the Moon to the shore of Lake Gregory, building private boat docks, a beautiful clubhouse and bathhouse and many other facilities for its members.

Lake Gregory has become the tourist attraction, water resource and property value enhancer that the original proponents envisioned.

CLUB SAN MORITZ: THE FIRST TWENTY YEARS

Club San Moritz Begins in 1939

The Club San Moritz began in the old Arrowhead Valley Club's lodge building in the Valley of the Moon (VOM) near the end of the Depression. The club was to be more than just a recreational facility or subdivision. The comprehensive project would include a water and land company, too. The success of Lake Arrowhead Village, with its property sales, may have influenced the new club's officers, as they had similar restrictive covenants in their deeds.

The club's history began in 1938, just after Lake Gregory was completed. The 1,200 acres of land around the new lake was for sale after the lawsuit between Arthur Gregory and Beth Cathcart was settled. The San Moritz/Lake Gregory Land and Water Company started as a California stock corporation on November 16, 1938, and then the corporation purchased the land, dividing it into thirty-two tracts of over 4,000 lots for future development. The Lake Gregory Water Company, a subsidiary of the land company would supply the water.

Club San Moritz was incorporated on December 20, 1939, as a California nonprofit corporation. It had the same corporate officers and directors as the Lake Gregory Water Company and the land company. The club's purpose was "to provide recreational and social activities for members, who were restricted by both Articles and Bylaws, to persons of good moral character and of a Caucasian Gentile race," according to Joe Rinnert, who was years later a president of the subsequent San Moritz Property Owners Association (SMPOA). Such ethnic restrictions were common for private clubs of that era. The Club San Moritz ideal was to create a recreational paradise, away from the city, in the pristine mountain air among the pines.

The first areas developed for purchase were the ABC tracts that were along Arosa Drive, near the Valley of the Moon. Lake Gregory Drive was not yet built, so the best access was from Twin Peaks, down Arosa Drive, as it had been since the 1920s. The previous road from Crestline to Valley of the Moon, through Huston Flats, had been flooded out by Lake Gregory.

An architectural design review board was established to promote the Swiss village theme. All building designs had to be approved by the architectural design review committee. Its stated intent was not to limit the varieties of style but to maintain a high building standard of quality alpine-style chalets. Many of those San Moritz chalet homes were well enough built to now be full-time homes.

The old lodge of the Arrowhead Valley Club in Valley of the Moon was completely remodeled, inside and out. The distinctive and massive fireplace was retained. The lodge's rustic log look was replaced with a shingle and rock Swiss-Alpine themed appearance.

Moon Lake, next to the clubhouse, was used as a private lake facility for canoeing, sunbathing and fishing, exclusively for club members.

The area was promoted as the "Alps of Southern California." The Club San Moritz made such an impact on the area that the post office in the Valley of the Moon changed its name from Moonlake to Switzerland, California, in May 1939. Consistent with the Swiss theme, the club commissioned longtime Crestline resident John Adams to build a spectacular entrance gate for the new community. Adams was a skilled stonemason and structural engineer, educated at Cal Poly San Luis Obispo.

At the entrance to the subdivision, Adams built, in 1939–40, what we nowadays call the Switzerland Monuments. On the western side of the

Club San Moritz opened in the remodeled Arrowhead Valley Club building in Valley of the Moon.

gates, the signs announce one's arrival at "Switzerland." When leaving the Club San Moritz property, the eastern side of the signs wish members a "Happy Return."

A comprehensive advertising campaign was undertaken, and Lake Gregory was soon well known throughout Southern California. The Crestline Chamber of Commerce and Charles S. Mann were also actively promoting the Crestline/Lake Gregory area.

Charles S. Mann saw potential and began the new Lake Gregory Village business district to tap into the new opportunities created by the lake and the club's members who might need things as they drove through Crestline to visit Club San Moritz.

The Club San Moritz was a private social club for people of good moral standing who had enough money to purchase land and build a Swiss-style chalet from the San Moritz Land and Water Company (SML&WC). Club San Moritz refurbished the large Valley of the Moon lodge building, with a restaurant and bar, where it continued the former tradition of weekly dances in the clubhouse.

The recently constructed Lake Gregory was just over the rise from the Club San Moritz. The road over the Lake Gregory dam was completed by the mid-1940s, and much to the disdain of Charles S. Mann and the

Crestline merchants, Lake Gregory Drive was created, connecting directly with the High Gear Road at Arrowhead Highlands. Now, Club San Moritz members could get to the club without driving through Crestline.

Club San Moritz Begins Its Love Affair with Lake Gregory

Lake Gregory was named after Arthur Gregory, who had subdivided the Valley of the Moon in the 1920s and spearheaded the building of Lake Gregory from 1935 to 1938. Lake Gregory had a 150-foot-wide reserve strip around its shores, which was open to the public as a free public shoreline.

In 1942, Club San Moritz (CSM) leased a section of the Lake Gregory reserve strip to use as private beachfront for club members' exclusive use and built a boat dock on the lake. The original 1942 five-year lease of the south shore was quite popular with club members. They enjoyed using the larger

Club San Moritz's new clubhouse was on the shore of Lake Gregory in the 1950s.

lake for boating and better fishing opportunities than the shallow Moon Lake, which sat next to their clubhouse.

The 1942 beach lease to Club San Moritz was superseded in 1947 by a twenty-five-year lease on a portion of the shoreline. The cost to the CSM for the reserve strip usage was to be $100 a month, from 1947 to 1952. Then the amount was to rise to $150 per month, from 1952 until January 1972. Then, the lease stated, another twenty-five-year option could be exercised for at least $100 per month, but not more than $200 per month, extending the exclusive use of the shore for CSM members until 1997. The CSM had definitely negotiated a very good lease for its members, which gave new members confidence in purchasing land and constructing chalets.

The 1940s were successful years for Club San Moritz. The CSM was profiting from its restaurant, bar, membership fees and gate fees. It charged one dollar for non–club members who wanted to use either Moon Lake or its leased section of shoreline at Lake Gregory. These peak years saw weekly dances and family activities.

The profits from the CSM allowed it to loan money to the SML&WC (at 2 percent interest) in the latter 1940s to purchase another 125 acres of land north of Huston Flat Road, which it subdivided and sold.

In 1950, Club San Moritz boasted a roster of five thousand members. Then, just four days before Labor Day 1950, the CSM lodge building in the Valley of the Moon burned to the ground.

The 1950s Began the Glory Years

The Club San Moritz was leasing seven and a half acres of land from the San Moritz Land and Water Company (easy to negotiate, since they had the same corporate officers) next to its leased south-end shoreline of Lake Gregory for $200 a month. There, between 1950 and 1952, it built the new Club San Moritz lodge building. Construction had already begun before the old lodge building burned. (This building is currently called the San Moritz Lodge).

The first part of the building, the restaurant and bar, was ready for use in the summer of 1951. Local trees, which were to be cut down for the widening and straightening of the roads and highways in the mountain area, were used to frame the building. Local rock was used in building the fireplaces, all giving the CSM significant savings in building material costs, yet it still cost $250,000 to build. It was designed to be the most beautiful building in the area.

Two views depict the beach club and new clubhouse, 1950s.

There was a waiting list of people who wished to become members of the Club San Moritz. It was exclusive, and it was the largest private club on the mountain, with many family activities and things for adults to do, as well.

The *Yodeler*, the club's monthly newspaper, wrote of year-round activities such as Easter egg hunts and Christmas celebrations, with every holiday having some event. Emphasizing the Swiss theme, it held yodeling and alpine costume contests. The summer activities included miniature golf, fishing, beach fun and boating, horseback riding and, of course, socializing with other CSM members. The CSM Pitch and Putt Golf Course and driving range in Valley of Enchantment was a new addition to the amenities offered to the members in the 1950s on the land the CSM had purchased from the Byron Waters Jr. family. The CSM was an active place, with many things occurring year round. The restaurant boasted renowned chefs with the best cuisine and hosted banquets celebrating every occasion.

The main lodge at Club San Moritz in its heyday.

Beginning in the early 1950s, those persons who purchased a qualifying lot from the San Moritz Land and Water Company received one of the limited 2,500 non–dues paying "life" memberships in the Club San Moritz. The Land Company paid the club a flat, one-time $150 fee (this short-sighted decision was the beginning of the end for the club).

The purchasers of property were required to qualify for membership in the club before being allowed to buy the property, as the deeds continued to be restricted to citizens "of the white-Caucasian race with good moral character." A background check was done on every potential property owner, including listing ancestry and their country of origin, and questioned if their family name had been changed since immigrating to the United States (it had not been that long since World War II).

The Club San Moritz's net income of $22,000 in 1954 increased significantly to $33,000 in 1955. Its net worth increased from $265,000 in 1954 to $299,000 in 1955. Its future looked rosy, encouraging more to want to join in the fun.

The San Moritz Property Owners Association (SMPOA) was organized in 1953 (just after the new clubhouse was completed). In 1956, the secretary of state registered the SMPOA as a fraternal order, reinforcing its ability to screen its membership.

The SMPOA was the successor to the Charter Life Members of the Club San Moritz from the Valley of the Moon days. One director was elected from each of the thirty-two tracts. The directors worked to protect the property values and to add more activities to the social calendar, including Mexican fiestas, Roaring Twenties events, Alpine Days, Monte Carlo Nights, amateur contests and the popular Saturday night teen dances. The new lodge at the CSM was the "happening place" on the mountain.

CONCLUSION

C restline was developed because of its location at the crest of Waterman Canyon and the many trees that grew in the forest. It first became a logging destination and then, because of the weather and scenery, a vacation destination. It has grown because of its beauty and those early development people who wanted to share it but also to protect it. The roads to the area have made it accessible, and the early developers wanted to keep it a scenic forested wonderland, different from the valley below. The road has been vastly improved and realigned three times over the years. This book has focused on Crestline on its first one hundred years, almost to the mid-twentieth century.

In the last sixty years, Crestline has continued to develop and grow. However, the town cannot expand its boundaries because the San Bernardino National Forest surrounds it. Inside its limits, the community has become more than just a vacation destination; it has become a community with many artistic elements, including theater, artists, music and more. Small businesses have developed to provide for the needs of its residents. It has generations of families who have chosen Crestline to be their home. To others, it has become a place to retire and escape the drudgeries of the crowded Southern California landscape. It is a quiet oasis in the middle of all that Southern California has become. It still faces the continual threat of destruction by wildfires, but with the development of the Crest Forest Fire Protection District, which was started in 1929, the community has remained safe. Those who call it home find it the perfect place to live, close to but still removed from the city.

CONCLUSION

There are many more stories that have been and can be told about Crestline and its surrounding mountain communities, such as the history of the Crest Forest School District, the Crest Forest Fire Department, the rest of the San Moritz story and the fear of devastation by the Panorama and Old Waterman Canyon fires, but the limits of this book have been exhausted, and those and other stories will need to be told another time.

People still ask the question: is it the altitude or the attitude that makes Crestline different? Most would agree, after learning about its unique history, that it's both.

ABOUT THE AUTHOR

Rhea-Frances Tetley's family developed the Valley of Enchantment section of Crestline beginning in 1924, and she has been visiting the area since birth. She has lived there with her family, full time, since 1976. She is a past president and founder of the Crest Forest/Rim of the World Historical Society and is currently on the board of directors of the Mountain History Museum in Lake Arrowhead, California.